The Absolute *Quickest Way to* Help Your Child *Change*

The Parenting Revolution Begins

The Absolute *Quickest Way to* Help Your Child *Change*

The Parenting Revolution Begins

Fred R. Lybrand Jr., *parent*

KAUFFMAN
BURGESS
P R E S S

The Absolute Quickest Way to Help Your Child Change

Published by Kauffman Burgess Press
Corsicana, Texas

ISBN 0-9652497-0-0
Parenting/Family

Printed in the United States of America.

2 3 4 5 6 7 – 00 99 98 97 96

*The writer does the most
who gives his reader the most knowledge
and takes from him the least time.*

Pos.— Sydney Smith

Contents

Dedication

To Jerrie S. Lybrand and Fred R. Lybrand Sr., my parents. Thank you for the love, example, and wisdom not to let us run your home when we were children. Also to Col. & Mrs. Donald L. White, Joanna's parents. Thank you for preparing and giving the world a daughter so committed to family.

Finally to the faithful members of Midland Bible Church, whose love, encouragement, and patience have helped forge my family, this work, and me.

Foreword

You hold in your hands a dangerous book. I began reading *The Absolute Quickest Way to Help Your Child Change* late one evening at bedtime, but I couldn't put it down until I finished it—at 2:00 in the morning! It is a wake up call that may keep you awake, with excitement for parenting.

That the modern family in America needs fixing is obvious. Hundreds of books have been written by highly trained professionals on fixing the home. Impressive psychological terms have been invented to label various family dysfunctions. Fixing these maladies can involve hours of counsel and years of effort, often with discouraging results. For many of us, parenting and fixing the home have become so complex and tiring, that we believe unless the experts do it, it can't be done.

As a marriage counselor, I know that the problems in our homes are usually not unconquerable. With God's help, the healing of our homes need not be wearisome either. Parents can solve their own challenges with some simple common sense marriage and parenting skills. Such is the emphasis of Fred Lybrand's work.

The Absolute Quickest Way to Help Your Child Change is succinct and readable. Fred provides a fresh perspective especially for individuals who feel helpless or lack the needed confidence in their parenting skills. While professionals have their place in family counseling, Fred provides a much needed emphasis that most parents can bring significant change within their families by themselves. He also gives you practical insights on how to do it. While Fred's solutions to parenting problems may appear simple, he is not at all simplistic. As a full time counselor, I find his easily understood formulas for the cause of family problems, si? => ie!, and the solutions to those problems ei! => si!, to be profound in their application. It works! I also liked Fred's emphasis on parents arriving at the right answers to their kid's problems by learning how to first ask the right questions.

Fred Lybrand feels that many parents often see no improvement because they never change their plan. Thankfully *The Absolute Quickest Way to Help Your Child Change* provides a roadmap which guides parents who are ready to risk traveling new paths towards improved marriage and family relationships. I know of no book so brief yet so full of wisdom and practical insight as this one.

Dr. Marlin Howe

HOPE FOR THE FAMILY
North Little Rock, Arkansas

Preface

Why would anyone write another book on parenting? And why would anyone dare call it revolutionary? If you continue to read, you will see that I am calling for a revolution of common sense in our country. My eight years as a parent and ten years as a pastor at Midland Bible Church in Midland, Texas, have overwhelmed me with one fact: **Parents need permission to parent.** There is a simple reason why parents have lost their permission and skill to parent in our country. We have lost our common sense to parent, and we've lost it because we have deferred our wisdom to so-called experts. Many of those experts will disagree with me. But are they disagreeing with me because I am wrong or because they are threatened?

My goal, however, is to be neither right, nor to threaten. Instead I want to return parenting from the bookshelves, radio stations, and counseling offices to its rightful home, Mom and Dad. There are a few central beliefs and secrets that all effective parents have known throughout time, secrets you'll know soon—but first you must answer one question...

1

Can Your Child Change?

It is a silly example. It hardly compares to the giants we parents face in these treacherous times—drugs, sex, disease, and violence—but it does demonstrate the principle well.

When our first-born son, Tripp, was only five years old, he had a nervous habit. It started out innocently enough; he would touch his ears and then his nose. In time, though, my wife, Joanna, began to worry about him. Tripp began to swat his ears, as you might to ward off a fly. He followed this by striking himself on the bridge of his nose. Swat, strike, swat, strike all day long.

Joanna is not one to panic, but this was too much. Naturally, as a dad, I was oblivious to the finer elements of compulsive head touching until she came and told me. She was concerned. He was beginning to bleed behind his ears and on his nose. Did he need counseling? What could cause such a problem? Was he trying to communicate some deep-seated emotional crisis within his five-year-old psyche?

One of the great secrets of child-rearing is knowing when to panic. Now was not one of those times. Panic alone can create more damage than imaginable. Instead, I opted to talk with Tripp. In a ten-minute conversation he was cured. Beginning with the next day we never saw the "tic" again. Better yet, it was Tripp who cured himself. My role was simply to help him change.

I am not a genius, nor is Tripp a grand exception among children (though, as parents we feel he's exceptional). I simply applied three fundamental convictions which I have used countless times as a pastor and father of four. Those convictions or beliefs are that children can change, I can help them change, and this change is greatly enhanced by following God's wisdom and the principles He originated.

I have applied these principles to all of our children, and they have paid off. For example, all of our children have slept through the night since they were six weeks old, none of them have ever had a temper tantrum, and when we say "come," "sit," or "go to bed," they do. Are they dogs? No, simply children who are well behaved because God has given their parents a measure of wisdom.

Some time ago we went shopping for furniture and took all the children with us (ages six, five, three, and one at the time). One store had a television set up with children's videos. Our kids watched a video while Joanna and I shopped. A few days later we returned to the store, and the salesperson who helped us said, "The whole office talked about your children all afternoon after you left. Your children were so good compared to the rest of the children we saw that afternoon. They really are precious."

Naturally, any parent would feel proud, but we know it is neither magic nor a set of "genetically" good children. Also, we would be dishonest if we did not admit a few struggles (for example, the time Tripp stabbed two friends with a mechanical pencil, or three-year-old Forrest tried out Ninja Aerobics on his Sunday School classmates). We also know nothing absolutely guarantees that our children will turn out well. But we are not fearful because we have a secret weapon: those three fundamental beliefs. I have no scientific proof or statistical data to support my assertion, but I am convinced that if parents do not start embracing these beliefs, then parenting will be torture instead of the pleasure it was meant to be.

Belief #1: My Child Can Change

All children can change. In fact, they are changing all the time. Your child has been changing since the moment of conception, not only physically, but emotionally, mentally, and spiritually as well. In a different light we call change growth. God designed our children to grow up, to mature. Everything we are doing as parents should be focused on helping them grow up healthy.

Change in itself is not necessarily good or bad; it is just different. As you look at your children and their need for change, what do you see? Are they trapped? Are they doomed to repeat their mistakes throughout life? Worse still, are they doomed to repeat your mistakes?

No! Your child can change because he can learn. Unfortunately, there are many parents who do not believe their child can do either. If you believe your child is terminally bad or a terminal liar, then you will help bring that belief about in that child. Your child may overcome that pessimism and prove you wrong, but why put him, her, or yourself through that when there is a better way. Believe your child can change, and watch him prove you right!

What would it take to convince you that your child can change? Statistics? Examples? A monolith treatise from an Ivy League scholar? Probably not. Two basic tools will convince you. The first is your own common sense. You know that your child can change since it is the nature of human beings to change. The second is experience. Just try the principles in this book and see if your child changes. You don't have to believe in the principles to try them. When you understand the ideas behind this belief, then try it. If your child changes, then you will have your evidence for the first belief and be well on your way to the second and third beliefs.

However, don't set yourself up for major disappointment by trying to take on a big challenge at first. Small wins are the training ground for confident learning. Learn how these principles work before applying them to a major challenge.

Belief #2: I Can Help My Child Change

The emphasis here is on "I can" or "we can" for couples. The first belief focuses on the child; the second focuses on you, the parent. If you are convinced that you cannot help your child, then you will not be able to offer him or her what is needed. Conversely, your child is convinced he can change you. He can talk, pout, or cry you into letting him stay up late, eating an extra dessert, or borrowing the car, depending on the age and hormones involved. Your child is scheming and planning. Your child a student of you, learning every counter move, and the exact location of every button that makes you say yes.

If your child doesn't give up so easily, why should you? If your child is older, then you should be able to think of many examples when you helped him change. Did you help your child color? Tie his shoes? Brush his teeth? Ask politely? If you believe he has forgotten these lessons, just watch how they all are applied to dating someday. You helped your child change in countless ways, and none of them are minor because in principle they are all the same. Helping a child change the way he asks for milk is no different than helping him give up thumb sucking or stop sneaking out at night. Whatever the age or challenge, you can still help your child change.

The proof, again, will be when you see it for yourself. Before then, keep in mind two important things. First, you control the learning environment until your child is on his own. The environment you create will help your child change. In fact, the way your child is today has a lot to do with the environment you helped create. If you change the environment, you help your child change.

The second important thing is that common sense can help you overcome the helplessness you sometimes feel toward your child. Often we feel helpless because we lack the proper equipment. Think about the last time you locked your keys in the car; didn't you feel overwhelmed and stupid and asked, "Now what do I do?" Most parents feel the same way. "Now what do I do?" The spare key for parenting is called common sense. You probably just forgot that you stuck it under the fender. In fact, the first sub-title for this book was, "how to help your child change, without your child's help." We'll see this phrase again, but in the meantime, remember; if your child could grow up without your help, then there would be no need for parents.

Belief #3: GOD CREATED A UNIVERSE GOVERNED BY PRINCIPLES

One of my favorite classic movies is *The Flight of the Phoenix*, starring Jimmy Stewart. He is a pilot whose plane has crashed in the desert, stranding him and his passengers. It is a story of survival, and fortunately one of the passengers is an engineer for an airplane company, who says they can build a new plane out of the wreck and fly to safety. They all agree and everything goes according to the engineer's plan until the others find out he works for a *model* airplane company. Talk about fear and second thoughts. The resolution comes when the engineer points out that aerodynamics is aerodynamics, no matter the size of the plane.

The same holds true with God: His principles work, no matter the problem. Whether you believe in God or not, He exists. Whether or not you believe in the principles He established for the universe, they exist too. Life is filled with marks of pain or joy from fighting against or cooperating with the way things work. My cousin Brian, when he was a small boy, believed he could run through a gasoline fire just like Superman. His belief that fire would not burn him did not square with reality, and he spent weeks in the hospital.

What about your approach to parenting? Have you been forcing your rules on a universe which will not listen? As surely as there are principles for flying and for flames, there are principles for parenting. The problem with most of us is that we have traded our common sense for consensus. We try to parent by following fads instead of studying truth. We are listening to so-called experts instead of God and His design for parents and children.

If I could show you exactly where to find the undeniable and foolproof answers to your parenting questions, would you study and apply them? I believe good parenting is as simple as understanding and applying the basic principles or fundamentals of good parenting. Every sport has fundamentals. When a golf shot strays into the gallery, some basic principle has been violated. When a tennis ball hits the net, a fundamental was overlooked. When a quarterback is sacked, a blocking assignment has been missed.

Why is parenting any different? We cannot make up our

own rules for this sport. Parenting is a serious responsibility and operates best when we follow the principles that govern it. Are there absolute guarantees? Hardly. Are there exceptions? Of course. Still, parenting is a part of this ordered universe God created, and if we follow the principles, the results will come.

The principles work because they square with reality. The difficulty of the problem does not matter. Problems are solved by applying basic principles. The examples and ideas you are about to learn may seem too simple, or not quite what you are wrestling with. Don't be fooled by simplicity. If the principles are true for something simple, then they will be true for more complex things.

But before we can help children change, we first need to start a revolution...

2

The Parenting Revolution

I propose a revolution. The nation is ripe, the people are hungry for it, and the clamor and call for revolutionaries to take up the banner for freedom is at an all-time high. The revolution I propose, and the one we need, is for common sense.

Common sense is the central theme and cornerstone of the principles we are studying. Our focus is parenting, but in America today common sense is an endangered species. Moreover, its foes are loaded with ammunition and a license to kill.

Who are the foes of common sense? Who is it that robs us of our freedom? The answer is experts. Experts do more to rip our freedoms from us than anything else. We quote experts. We defer to experts. We idolize experts. We even scurry uphill to stand next to them, and occasionally, we become one ourselves.

The existence of an expert means the rest of us are, at best, novices and laymen. We are taking on a grave responsibility when we are acting on our own ideas instead of an expert's. If you are not an expert, then you are probably not qualified to make solid decisions in a given area. Confidence erodes as experts arise.

Consider a few examples: stockbrokers, teachers, Ph.D.s, consultants, physicians, lawyers, clergy, psychologists. What once was the domain of many, is now the domain of few. We can't manage our finances; we need an expert. We can't look after our health; physicians must. We can't just shake hands; our lawyer must put it on paper. We can't teach our children; that's a teacher's job. There are even specialists that businesses hire to fire their employees properly.

"How can you, in all fairness, make such a blanket judgment on experts?" you may ask. Please don't misunderstand. We certainly can't avoid the need for experts in certain areas. If I am having eye surgery or being audited by the IRS, then I want a specialist with me all the way. Surgery and taxes, though, aren't the same as parenting. As I stated in Chapter 1, there is some order to this universe which God created, and parenting is no exception. God created parents to be the guardians and protectors of children; not the state and not social services. God, or even nature if you prefer, doesn't tend toward random foolishness. God would no more give children to parents without the potential to parent than He would give the eagle wings with no impulse to fly.

Already, you probably have realized that I have created a paradox. You likely are reading this book hoping that as an expert I can help you with parenting. But I just challenged the value of experts. The result? You can stop reading right now. I am not a parenting expert and don't promote myself as one. But I am a parent, and that is the essence of the Parenting Revolution: as a parent, you are the God-intended expert for your own child. If you are interested in common sense and a few insights from a fellow parent, then read on. If you want statistical milieu and longitudinal studies, then you'll need to look elsewhere. Similar to Elton Trueblood's thought that Christianity is "one beggar showing another beggar where to find bread," I too am talking to you parent to parent, common sense to common sense.

Experts, on the other hand, undermine common sense and the areas to which common sense best applies. Common sense, rare despite its name, is common because it is available to everyone. Whenever you find an expert, then you have found someone with information that is not widely available. Think about parenting skills. If there are parenting experts, then the rest of us don't know what the experts do? In that same line, if we knew what the experts did, then they wouldn't be experts anymore.

My concern is that if we don't start a revolution, the privilege of parenting may be taken away. Experts eventually might declare us incompetent to parent and take our children from us. This Expert Syndrome creates a deadly cycle. We lose our confidence because experts disagree with our common sense (for example, some experts wrongly say spanking of any kind will damage a child for life). Without confidence, we quit thinking and exercising our common sense. Without exercise, common sense becomes extinct. Finally, without our common sense, we become defenseless and simply conclude we don't know what we're doing. We are left looking feverishly for a magazine or a talk show that will give us expert advice with which to experiment on our children. Trial and error is no way to parent.

The amazing thing is that you already have everything

you need to become a good parent. Most of us have been wandering around like we are in Oz, looking for a wizard who magically will send us back to Kansas, and the whole time we are wearing the ruby slippers. We need to return the confidence and joy to parenting that has so forcefully eroded through the years. We need to enlist an army to reclaim the most powerful of parenting tools: our common sense.

HOW TO GET MORE COMMON SENSE

"Common sense" can mean two things. It can refer to the general knowledge for living within a culture—an example might be that everyone knows you don't go into certain parts of a city after dark—or it can refer to the idea that common sense is wisdom, which is central to our discussion.

Wisdom is what we need for effective parenting; it is what we need for results. Often we think of wisdom as the sole possession of a sage on a secluded mountaintop, which supports the Expert Syndrome. The sage sits above us all, disjointed from the real world. Wisdom is not meant for sages alone, but for all of us who seek it.

Actually, wisdom is truth. More specifically, wisdom is applied truth concerning the results of life choices.[1] Wisdom says that if an individual constantly adds to his debt, then he will become enslaved to his creditors as interest multiplies. Wisdom also says that the person who lives within his means and saves will become prosperous as the funds multiply. The difference between the two is that one ignores the truth, while the other properly applies it. Our definition then expands: **Wisdom is properly applied truth concerning the results of life choices.** Wisdom is knowing and making the right decisions about life.

So, how do we get wisdom? I believe there is only one thing required to get wisdom; you must make a lifelong decision to pursue it. "That's it, just pursue wisdom? Doesn't everybody want wisdom?" No, they really don't. The alcoholic is in pursuit of pleasure, or more accurately, less pain; however misguided that feeling may be. He is not after wisdom, just another drink. Sexually promiscuous individuals are not pursuing wisdom. Although they know the consequences, many take no precautions and risk disease and even death. Even the person in debt is looking for temporary happiness, ignoring the pain that will come with the bills. Everybody may think they want wisdom, but not many will pay the price.

The Book of Proverbs has always been revered as the greatest collection of wisdom in the Bible. But it is more than just a collection of wise sayings. Assume for a moment that wisdom, as we've defined it, forms a single essence like light. We see and use light every day for many things. Light, however, is not simply "light." Instead, it can be divided into various colors, which blend to make light "white." To see the full spectrum of light, we can simply take a prism and shine light through it. The prism, in bending the light, reveals the colors of the rainbow.

Proverbs is like a prism. The many components of wisdom are gloriously displayed as they pass through the book. Proverbs was given as a "starter kit" for those who desire to pursue wisdom. Take a moment to reflect carefully on Proverbs 8.

Wisdom Calls All Men
"Does not wisdom cry out,
And understanding lift up her voice?
She takes her stand on the top of the high hill,
Beside the way, where the paths meet.
She cries out by the gates, at the entry of the city,
At the entrance of the doors:"
To you, O men, I call,

And my voice is to the sons of men.
O you simple ones, understand prudence,
And you fools, be of an understanding heart." (Prov. 8:1-5)

Wisdom Is the Way of Righteousness

"Listen, for I will speak of excellent things,
And from the opening of my lips will come right things;
For my mouth will speak truth;
Wickedness is an abomination to my lips.
All the words of my mouth are with righteousness;
Nothing crooked or perverse is in them.
They are all plain to him who understands,
And right to those who find knowledge." (Prov. 8: 6-9)

Wisdom Is to Be Pursued Above Everything

"Receive my instruction, and not silver,
And knowledge rather than choice gold;
For wisdom is better than rubies,
And all the things one may desire cannot be compared
with her." (Prov. 8:10-11)

Wisdom Is a Partner of Morality

"I, wisdom, dwell with prudence,
And find out knowledge and discretion.
The fear of the LORD is to hate evil;
Pride and arrogance and the evil way
And the perverse mouth I hate.
Counsel is mine, and sound wisdom;
I am understanding, I have strength." (Prov. 8:12-14)

Wisdom Brings Success

"By me kings reign,
And rulers decree justice.
By me princes rule, and nobles,
All the judges of the earth.

I love those who love me,
And those who seek me diligently will find me.
Riches and honor are with me,
Enduring riches and righteousness.
My fruit is better than gold, yes, than fine gold,
And my revenue than choice silver.
I traverse the way of righteousness,
In the midst of the paths of justice,
That I may cause those who love me to inherit wealth,
That I may fill their treasuries." (Prov. 8:15-21)

In many ways Proverbs 8 is the theme of the entire book. Wisdom is likened to a woman calling out for companionship. She boasts of many benefits to any suitor, especially that she can belong to anyone. These verses hold a great promise for those who pursue wisdom. In particular notice verse 17: *"I love those who love me, And those who seek me diligently will find me."*

Wisdom has made us a promise. If we love wisdom and seek wisdom, then we will find it. We can state the principle: **The one becoming wise, pursues wisdom.** It is a lifelong adventure. It is also an upwards pursuit. We don't get wise and quit. We get wise and get wiser still. George Washington Carver who found over three hundred uses for peanuts, etc., is credited with observing, "Anything will give up its secrets if you love it enough."

How true for wisdom. How true for parenting. When we love our children enough and long for the wisdom to rear them in the best of all possible ways, it is then we begin to make sense, common sense. When we seek wisdom as others do wealth (Prov. 2:4; 8:10-11), then we will acquire wisdom. We are not told how or when, but we are assured of finding it.

The old adage is, "When the student is ready, the teacher appears." This doesn't mean the teacher was absent; the student was. Unless we are willing to learn, we can see neither truth nor the teacher who brings it. Common sense has abandoned us as parents because we quit pursuing it. Instead, we have pursued experts and turned our children into experiments. It is time to regain our common sense, it is time to revolt.

Are you ready for some common sense? It requires only an initial decision: to pursue wisdom for life. If you love her enough, she will tell you her secrets. Indeed, she's already openly told us many of them in Proverbs. What's keeping you from deciding right now to make wisdom and common sense a lifelong pursuit? What's keeping you from joining the Parenting Revolution?

THE PROBLEM WITH PROBLEMS

Imagine you are a common sense parent. The time you have spent pursuing wisdom has paid off. Your children, while not perfect, are turning out well. Problems come, but they are conquered. Others have noticed the change. "Your children are so well behaved," they say. "You must be so proud." You blush and dismiss the compliment saying, "Oh, we're just lucky. It's genetics. We were given kids we couldn't mess up."

That's how I facetiously respond because we, as parents, amazingly want credit when our children are good, but pass out blame when they are bad: faulty genes, too much sugar, brain waves, the schools, society, and even the stars for the astrological parent. Of course there really are challenges with our children that are beyond our control. But a challenge is something to overcome, not an excuse for our child's behavior. My family understands challenges. Joanna grew up dyslexic, Tripp has cerebral palsy, and I'm 5-foot-6 (on a good day).

But as a common sense parent you don't blame and you face challenges. Because of your success with your children, friends have dropped by to get some advice about their four-year-old son, Jeffrey. (Generally when people get to the point of asking for help from fellow parents, they are in a good bit of misery; respect them for how much courage it takes even to ask!)

Jeffrey has taken to throwing tantrums. Naturally, the big one that day occurred at the grocery store. The cart was half full and things were going well until Jeffrey was able to grab a can of smoked oysters in one of Mom's unguarded moments. Your friend asked Jeffrey very nicely to "give the smoked oysters to Mommy." He refused, and when Mommy took them away, Jeffrey had a conniption. He screamed and cried and yelled like a fledgling actor in a cheap horror movie. Your friend tried to hush Jeffrey, even giving him back the smoked oysters (and two alternate brands), but Jeffrey threw them on the floor and continued his public storm. Your friend's only recourse, after trying to buy him off with candy and clapping her hand over his mouth, was to leave the store posthaste. Incidentally, your friends also have invited themselves to stay for supper because nothing awaits them at home.

What's the problem here, common sense parent? Before you advise too quickly, let me remind you of the importance of understanding the problem. Sound advice for the wrong problem is not very sound advice. How can you determine what Jeffrey's problem is and what is causing it? How can you be sure your guess is the right one? There is a way to know, but you must first understand the nature of problems. If you don't understand that, you probably won't solve your own problems or anyone else's.

PROBLEMS ARE NOT SIMPLE

The problem with problems is complexity. Problems are not simple, although solutions can be. Problems are rarely comprised of one ingredient, therefore, if we jump too soon we may not offer a successful solution.

Another example. You have been asked to join a task force to help solve the traffic problem in Houston, Texas. The leader of the task force calls the meeting to order and writes a simple question on the white board in large red letters: "What is the problem with the traffic in Houston?" After thirty minutes of brainstorming, you and your coworkers offer the following list of problems: too many cars, too many people, too many people driving alone, not enough roads, too many downtown businesses, poor emergency medical access to accidents, bottlenecks and rubbernecks, too much through traffic on I-10, businesses releasing people at the same time, population explosion beyond planning, (again) not enough roads, speed limits.

Can we really say there is a single problem? What if the task force decided the only real problem was too many people? That might lead to making sure that people quit moving to the city and that a few hundred thousand others moved away. How about speed limits? Changing them may be the answer, but allowing faster travel would likely cause more serious wrecks. Are you beginning to see the problem with problems...and hasty solutions?

As I said, problems are complex. Beyond the complexity, however, is the fact that we tend to find solutions for the single problem we see. **If we don't see the complexity, we don't truly see the problem.** An illustration of the complexity issue has to do with weathermen. Some years ago a meteorologist offered the "butterfly effect" to explain why weathermen are so consistently wrong. He observed that weather in one area is affected by the various weather systems all over the world. He said, in effect, "a butterfly fluttering in Tokyo can cause a tornado in Tennessee."

The last thing any common sense parent wants to do is

to attempt to fix the wrong part of a problem. But, we can be strategic. There is a better way to approach problems; learn to be solution or result centered. First, settle it in your mind that deciding what the problem is will not really help. Remember little Jeffrey. What is his problem? Does Jeffrey have a tantrum gene? Is he afraid of smoked oysters? Should he just not go to grocery stores? Is it Mommy and Daddy? Was he just tired and hungry? Could Jeffrey be going through a phase and will it leave him before he asks for his first raise? The list goes on.

Common sense looks beyond the problem to the solution. Unless there are extraordinary circumstances, Jeffrey can be helped and he will never have tantrums again. In fact, there is a proverb that we will learn that says he was actually taught to have a tantrum. Helping Jeffrey really is just common sense. If common sense will cure a tantrum, it will cure most other behavior issues with your child, regardless of age.

Before we can answer the troubling questions about our children and help them change, however, we must learn about one of our greatest weapons for facing life's challenges. We must learn the lesson of the Village...

3

Are You Asking the Right Questions?

THE VILLAGE: A PARABLE

A young man lived in a small village, and he had a gift. He could run.

In this country athletics was revered and esteemed as a way to fame and honor, for both the young man and his village. Even though he liked to run and did well, something was still wrong. He won some races, but lost others. Sometimes he even stopped before the end of the race because he would just get too tired to finish.

Everyone knew he had great potential, but no one seemed to know what was wrong. The young man thought he knew the answer, but never told anyone for fear of ridicule. He believed he just wasn't motivated enough. Sure he loved to run and it felt "right" when he was in the race. But soon he would tire. The races he finished always had the same ingredient; he made himself finish. "Just one more mile," he'd say as he coaxed his body to endure. "No pain, no gain!" he'd huff when he practiced. Still, he just couldn't find enough motivation to really run his best. Deep down he knew it was in him to run with the wind, but he just couldn't find the way to make his outside match his inside.

One day a visitor came through the Village. He was a Man of Prudence who traveled the villages and towns to offer insight as his service to God and as his means of survival. His work began with the greatest problem, which if he solved it, obligated the village to provide for him as long as he stayed. The Man of Prudence never demanded others to follow his wisdom nor did he defend himself, his only goal was to suggest an answer. He also never solved a problem without being first asked. He truly was wise.

The Village was excited; the last Man of Prudence to visit them was only remembered by the oldest members of the Village, who were children when he lived among them. The Village was also excited because the wisdom of a Man of Prudence lived on with the people and prospered the village for many, many years.

The Village Council met to decide which problem to give to the Man of Prudence, knowing that it must be the greatest of all their problems. The Council had been careful to preserve the Parchment of Instruction, which reminded them of the standard for a true problem: A true problem, worthy of another's wisdom, is one incurable by time and asked only when an unquestioned willingness to accept a true answer abides within.

When the Council read and reflected together on the Parchment, they agreed that the small grain harvest did not qualify, since each season was its own and next year would be different still. They also knew that replacing the fifth Council member who had traveled now beyond life was also wrong, since no Village member was yet ready to take his place.

Clearly, the Village Runner was the most confounding problem. Time had not solved the problem and age would eventually slow him all the more. They also agreed to be willing to try any solution the Man of Prudence suggested.

The Village and Council gathered for the historic day, which would be retold to generations. After hearing the matter, the Man of Prudence asked the Runner how he had sought to solve the problem. The young man hung his head. From the crowd someone yelled, "It is our fault. We should be blamed for not cheering enough." Another shouted, "No, it is the Council's fault. They have the wealth of the Village and could provide a better opportunity to train."

Although the whole village was stirred, the Man of Prudence was unmoved. "And what does he say for himself?" the wise one asked.

"I have sought to blame the Village and the Council, but it is not their fault. I also found myself accusing my competition of cheating, or wishing I had grown up in the cities from which they came. 'If I had only had their advantages, I could run with the wind as is in my heart,' I thought bitterly and alone. Alas, I have admitted that it is my fault. I am not motivated enough. I lack commitment and desire. I love to run, but I have accepted that I do not love to run enough. Unless you, Man of Prudence, can pour greater desire into me, then I can only live in the disgrace of my failure."

The Village was divided. Many were saddened and sought to comfort the young man by blaming themselves all the more. Others spit, "I knew it," and wagged their heads in disgust at the Runner.

The Man of Prudence only smiled. It was the smile the Village would learn to love. It was the smile of solution, which the Man of Prudence could not restrain whenever the moment came finally to reveal the answer. "The difference," he said, "between a problem and a solution is that you understand the solution."

The wise man paused to let his words sink in, then asked, "Why would a cliff-diver always beat a runner in a race to the water?"

The Village and the Man of Prudence were now in a duel of silence. Softly, one voice said, "It is unfair. They race in different ways."

The Man of Prudence responded, "Thank you for speaking, and you are right. Yet, the difference is not only in the way they race, but in what stands between each man and the water."

A member of the Council spoke up, "The path down the cliff is not in the way of the diver, therefore he must win!"

"Exactly," said the Man of Prudence. "It is in the young man to run with the wind, but something is between him and the wind he chases."

"I must learn to dive to the water...I mean wind...instead of run down the path on the cliffs?" the Runner stated and asked at the same time.

"Exactly!" the Man of Prudence almost interrupted. "You have been seeking to create something in you that is already there. Instead, you must look to what hinders you. The path is in the way, but you can only see the path as the right way to race. One day a runner won the race to the water because he saw the path as a hindrance not as a help.

"Haven't you," he continued, "merely seen yourself as needing to try harder on the path? Haven't you sought to blame instead of understand?"

No answer was needed as he went on.

"What stands between you and the wind? For all of us except the young ones who admire you, both desire and ability stand between us and the wind. Desire and ability you have."

The Village nodded and gathered closer as the Man of

Prudence asked the Runner again, "What stands between you and the wind?"

The young man stared at his feet but had no guesses. "Tomorrow I shall answer," said the Man of Prudence, "but first the young man must wrestle the night, it is his teacher for now."

The young man did wrestle.

Through the night he ran again in every race. He saw every runner and every victory and every defeat. "What stands between me and the wind?" The question echoed in his head. There was no answer. The wind was just too fast for him. Finally, he resigned himself to a fitful sleep.

The next day when the Village and Council gathered again the young man was missing.

"Find him," the Man of Prudence said.

Soon he came running to the assembly with apologies and sleepy eyes. "I am sorry for my lateness, but I know the answer!" The Village listened with one heart. "I was sleeping the deep sleep that follows a solution," the Runner explained. "I know what stands between me and the wind." There was no question in his voice.

"Go ahead," the Man of Prudence beamed.

"I feel a threat in speaking," he said. "Just as the cliff-diver of your example must have shocked the crowd by leaving the path, I fear that I too will shock my family and friends. I fear too the Council will chasten me."

"Fear not," said the Man of Prudence. "If you are right and they will not hear you, then this village is not yet ready for wisdom. The test each village must offer a Man of Prudence is a test of the village more than the Man. Answer, and we will see with which quill history will write."

The Runner drew a breath and let it collect in his whole body. "These stand between the wind and me," he said as he pointed to his legs. His legs had the traditional, if not ornate, *chains and shackles of the Village.* "Please hear me," he said. "I love the Chains of Remembrance and have worn them with honor since my thirteenth summer, but they are the path in the cliff-diver's way. I am faster than the wind, and I have a heart to run. The wind has speed, but no heart. It only races, but I can race with intention. The wind defeats me because the wind wears no Chains of Remembrance. If you will shackle the wind I shall catch it. If you unshackle me I will become the wind in every race. No other runner wears these chains. I race down the path while they dive through the air."

The Village was indeed shocked.

"But," began the Council leader. "We have worn these chains for ten generations. Grandfathers and grandmothers we cannot name wore these chains. It is our way to remember our freedom. Our ancestors were slaves. They suffered horribly and with final freedom began this tradition for our remembrance and for those to follow us. It is forbidden. It cannot be for even a Village hero to walk in public without them. What can we do Man of Prudence, we have no choice."

The Man of Prudence smiled again. "Is it not as I said, the difference between a problem and a solution is that you understand the solution? The young man longs for freedom, but the chains make him a slave. Did your forebearers really intend for you to remember freedom by adding more slavery?"

The Village thought with one mind as the Man of Prudence continued.

"The Chains of Remembrance were unquestioned until today, hence they were seen as Truth. The path as the only way to the water was also unquestioned, thus was also seen as Truth. Have you not confused the chains with the thing to remember? Have you not created a new slavery in the name of freedom?

"The wise never make a Truth bow to equal the paper the Truth is written on. The wise also do not accept anything as Truth without question unless a Truth rests under it. The wise know that a Truth can withstand any assault, therefore the wise do not defend Truth. Also, the wise seek and accept change when new understanding pleads for change. Only the wise know that Truth is never the source of hurt, but of help."

The Village accepted the Man of Prudence, or rather, he accepted the Village. The Village Council chose to exchange the chains for a single anklet, reserving the Chains of Remembrance for ceremonies and celebrations. The memory of freedom was preserved, and the young man brought fame and honor to the Village as he and the wind left the other runners to ponder, "What stands between me and the wind?"

WHAT STANDS BETWEEN US AND THE WIND?

As with any parable, "The Village" has many applications. Certainly all of us relate to the sense of being motivated inside, but restrained outside. We want to do something, but we can't seem to find permission to do it. Isn't this like our parenting? We want to influence our children toward honor, goodness, and contribution. We want them to make a difference in this world, and yet, we seem restrained. How do we parent effectively? It is time, if you've committed to wisdom, for your own chains to come off.

The lesson to learn from this story is about problem solving. The Man of Prudence led the villagers to a solution. How did he do it? He merely helped them ask the right questions. **The difference between common sense parents and the rest is found largely in the questions they ask.** The Parenting Revolution is dependent on asking revolutionary questions.

The Runner and the Village had quit asking questions except one, "What is wrong with the Runner?" The conclusion was that he wasn't trying hard enough. The Man of Prudence instead had the Runner ask a new question, "What stands between you and the wind?" It was in that question that the Runner found his own answer.

Why do questions make a difference? Indeed, what is it that is so important about questions? If you'll stop right now, you'll notice yourself thinking about the questions I have asked. If you begin to think, then you will begin to develop common sense.

What stands between us and the wind as parents? I have offered a number of things so far, but I have especially focused on experts. Don't experts make up a large portion of the chains we wear? How do experts interfere with our common sense parenting? I believe experts tempt us to quit thinking. Who can argue with an expert? Don't they know best? Before long we stop thinking altogether. The expert will think for us. We should not ask questions, we should just do what we're told to do. Please don't hear these criticisms as blaming the experts, they are not the problem. We parents are the problem. When we quit asking the right questions and quit thinking, then the experts are the only ones left thinking.

There is an exception to the Expert Syndrome, and I encourage listening with discernment to this exception. The exception is what we might call, the Permission Giving Expert. There are a few experts on our side out there. They are experts in parenting who believe in us as parents. They exist to help us think and to solve our own problems as parents. These experts do not tell us what to do, they motivate us to think and grow in our own common sense. These experts are like the Man of Prudence.

ARE YOU ASKING THE RIGHT QUESTIONS?

In his book, *What a Great Idea?*, Charles Thompson relates an example of asking the right questions from Thomas MacAvoy, former president and chief operating officer of Corning Glass Works:

> One day, while MacAvoy was a senior chemist in a lab at Corning, Corning's president said to the head of

research, 'Glass breaks. Why don't you do something about that?' The directive to the lab then became: 'We're going to prevent glass from breaking.' The lab came up with twenty-five different ways of preventing glass from breaking; eighteen of them worked, and five made money.

The most interesting aspect of this exchange is not what the president did ask but what he did not ask. He did not ask 'Why does glass break?' That question might have produced months of exhaustive research, resulting in some highly scientific reports, which would collect dust on a shelf. Instead, the boss went straight for the desired solution: How can we make glass that doesn't break? The end result was the now-famous Correlle line of dinnerware.[2]

Do you remember the point from Chapter 1 about an ordered universe operating by principles? The proper use of questions is another one of these principles. **Right solutions follow right questions.** You may solve a problem with poor questions, but it won't happen often. If you read no farther, at least learning to ask better questions about your child's behavior will bring about change...dramatic change.

Consider an example. Your teenager comes home one day and has decided on a crew cut on one side of his head and a ponytail on the other. Additionally, he has decided to quit using all odor restraining applications (soap, deodorant, cologne, etc.) because it's just "being fake" and he wants to "be real." Moreover, he only wants to eat cactus because, as a desert plant, it has the essential ingredients of survival in it.

What questions would you be asking yourself about your child? I know several come to mind. Some of you might even skip the questions to move straight to the answers! What if you asked this, "How am I going to get through this stage until he outgrows it?" Wouldn't the only solutions available have to do with you? Would the question of your enduring a stage ever lead to a way to help your child change? No, it never would.

There are other, more strategic questions to ask. If you learn to ask them, and a few more you will pick up along the way, you will find dramatic differences in your parenting, as well as your emotions. Why don't you first begin by adding this question to your life, "If I stick with this question I'm asking, what kind of answers am I limited to?" Try it on your most recent trial. What questions have you been asking?

Let me give you a last challenge about questions. One mother asked me why people don't ask the right questions more often. I gave her a number of reasons: lack of wisdom, lack of teaching, an abundance of assumptions that keep us from asking questions ("all glass breaks and nothing can be done about it"), and perhaps just plain ignorance.

Nothing, however, stands in our way of asking life-changing questions more than fear. Many of us are scared to think. Many of us don't want to face our own responsibility for how things are; it's easier just to steer clear of those kinds of questions. Many of us don't want to look stupid, so we don't ask "stupid" questions. Most of all, I believe we intuitively know that asking the right questions will lead us to change, and many of us are scared to death to change. It takes courage to ask the right questions.

One final question. If the change would bring you greater joy, happiness, and fulfillment, would it not then be worth it to change? If you say "yes," great! But there is still something you desperately need to become a common sense parent and join the revolution. It is a special knowledge that used to be widely known, but is now largely forgotten by most parents. It has been hidden, but now you'll know it as...

4

The Common Sense Secret

What do we mean when we say we know a secret? Often, it simply means we have information that is not to be shared with others. If you have ever tried to have a family surprise party and told your children under five to "keep it a secret," then you know the challenge of secrets. The idea of secrets intrigues us. It is as though we long for special knowledge that will allow us to be ahead of others. At the same time, there is a desire to share these secrets broadly and openly when they will benefit those we love and mankind at large.

Antonio had a secret. During his lifetime from 1644 to 1737, he developed a craft. The craft was to make musical instruments. In making the instruments, however, it became important to concoct a glue or resin that would carry each note perfectly from the mind of the musician, through the violin, and to the audience. Antonio was successful. Today, the most prized violins in the world are called by his name, Stradivarius. These violins are mysterious and prized because Antonio left the violins, but took the secret of his glue and how he made his instruments to his grave.

We are not concerned here with music, but with parenting. The parallel though should be clear. The harmony and beauty that true music offers this world is like the child who grows up well. The child who grows up to add richly to the world as an extension of the efforts of his mother and father is their "gift" to the world. Other children, sadly, do not contribute to the world, but instead take from the world. These individuals, as they grow and do harm among us, are as apparent and unnerving as an untuned piano in a black tie symphony. There are secrets to parenting, especially to common sense parenting. There are secrets that are essential to the Parenting Revolution.

These secrets, however, are not to be hidden under lock and key or taken to the grave with us. Instead, they are to be proclaimed, taught, and promoted. They are not intended by God to be secrets. The secret of common sense parenting is not a secret because it has been hidden, but because it has been forgotten. We have an opportunity to reclaim and share these secrets in our revolution. And as with any revolution, the truth is the greatest weapon in the hands of a common and united people. Like no other revolution, this one must be a grassroots revolution; a revolution in the family, a revolution from the parents of this generation to the future parents of the next generation.

THE COMMON SENSE
SECRET IN THREE PARTS

In an honest moment, haven't you seen another family that seems to make things work and has exemplary children? In this honest moment, didn't you toy with the question, "I wonder how they do it?" Deep down we all know it is not luck or a fortunate draw from the genetic pool of humanity. Instead, it is just as you suspected. These parents know something that you do not. Now, we cannot reduce the complexity of human personality and child-rearing to a few simple formulas and techniques; to do so, in itself, goes against wisdom. We can, however, learn something from parents who are effective in their parenting.

The great mistake we make when we look at effective parents is to attempt to do what they do without thinking what they think. Whenever we try to change our lives by simply changing our actions, we create a great internal struggle. It has been known for the ages that people generally act consistently with how they think. When people are changed, it is largely because their thinking has been changed. Surely, you have noticed how you begin to think about something, and think about it more, and think about it more. The moment finally arrives when you can no longer simply think; you must act. Anybody who has ever proposed marriage to another has experienced this. We can't continue to seriously think about getting married without actually getting married.

Some years ago, a conference speaker shared the following. He, as a Christian, was being trained to share the good news with others. He was concerned though about forcing his beliefs on uninterested "victims." Indeed, the balance is delicate between sharing a message of eternal importance and offending people with the way we communicate. During this training, he was in a large city and saw a person standing on a street corner handing out tracts about Christianity. It was all he could take. Suddenly, in a moment, he saw this person as hindering the cause of Christ. This person was "hassling" people. This person was intruding on others' daily lives and forcing on them information they had not requested. This person was a problem that he aimed to fix. He stormed up to the man passing out the tracts and gave him a "piece of his mind that he could not afford to lose." After rebuking this poor man and explaining the damage he was doing, he paused for a response. The response was simply a few strained grunting sounds. The man passing out the tracts was mute. He could not speak. He could not talk. He could not communicate with language. Instead, from his heart, he wanted others to know the loving God he served. The best way he had found to do it was to hand out tracts, which said in ink what he could not say with his tongue.

How would you have felt if you had attacked this person. How will you now think about people handing out tracts for the rest of your life? If you are like me, you will be more cautious about judging others. Now, our concern is not about being judgmental, but rather how thinking affects actions. This conference speaker, from that moment on, began to think differently about people who are engaged in sharing their faith.

If you are going to become a common sense parent, then you must first learn to think like common sense parents think. **Perhaps the greatest mistake in most of the books on parenting is to show parents what to do and not how to think.** My hope is to change that trend and to challenge you to begin thinking differently about parenting. I know there are dozens of principles and beliefs that go into good parenting. However, as you pursue wisdom, you will discover them for yourself. For now, I want to help you get started because I believe there are three other basic beliefs that true common sense parents hold. If you will begin to make these beliefs central to your parenting, then you will likely see dramatic changes in your child.

Before we begin, let me make one suggestion. Write these principles on a 3 x 5 card and take them with you for a week. Think about them in as many ways as you can. Find some friends who might sit and talk about these principles to help clarify each other's understanding. In any way possible, focus your mind fully on these keys so they can be driven deeply into your soul. It will be natural to experience resistance. It will be normal for you to say "that's not true," but it is those other beliefs that have produced the results you have so far. If you want to see your child change, then those beliefs must be replaced by these three new ones. You might keep asking yourself this one question, "What if this secret is really true?" A helpful shortcut may even be to pray about these principles. Open your life to God, and let Him emblazon them on your heart.

Finally, each of these parts is important. They make up a whole and cannot be taken separately. You will not experience the true power of common sense unless you embrace all three.

1. The Parent Has the Advantage over the Child

The most important question every new parent must ask and answer is, "Who will run this home?" Sadly, in our day, many parents have given up the control of the home to the children. Everything revolves around the children. The deepest concern is to make sure the children are "happy" and well pleased with Mommy and Daddy. If you have fallen into this trap, you must realize it is the opposite of common sense. It is also no wonder that when the children finally "leave the nest" that so many couples find great difficulties in adjusting. It is also no wonder that many children in our day are invited to come home and live there well into their thirties. If you have fallen into this hole, you can still get out, but first you must remember the first rule of holes: when you find yourself in a hole, quit digging. Your children may run your home, but it is only by your permission. *You* have the advantage over your child.

There are four reasons why you have the advantage over your child. First, from common sense, we know you are smarter than your child. Now, this may change with age, but especially in the early years, a child cannot know more about life than a parent. You know that stoves burn and electricity shocks. You know that cars kill and plastic suffocates. You have been placed in the life of your child to teach him these things, not to hoard them as secrets. You have the advantage because you have more knowledge than your child.

The second reason deals with volition, which means that you can act. Whether or not you have ever paused to think about it, you have the ability to make choices in your life. Children, on the other hand, are in the process of learning to make choices. Especially, when they are younger, children mostly react to what is going on around them. You, as a parent, do not have to react, but you can act. A sudden noise can frighten a child and cause him to cry. You also might be startled by the sound, but you can make the choice not to cry, to run away, to investigate the noise, or to evaluate and ignore it. A child will be prone just to cry and cling to you. You are not only smarter than your child, but you have a greater freedom to consider and select from the choices available. Your child, for the most part, reacts to what is going on around him.

The third reason the parent has the advantage is a spiritual one. God has given parents the leverage and the power to influence. Throughout the Bible, parents are instructed to train their children and are seen as accountable before God as stewards of these small lives placed in their hands. In part, this is why we see becoming a parent as such a great responsibility. We know through our common sense that we will have the greatest influence on the lives of our children than possibly any other human being. With this responsibility comes ability. If you leave a teenaged babysitter with a toddler and return home to find the entire contents of your refrigerator creatively decorating your walls, who do you blame? You may be tempted to blame the child, but it's the babysitter's fault for allowing the toddler to redecorate. The babysitter is older and should be more responsible, and has the ability to keep the child from misbehaving. The babysitter is accountable for the actions of the child because the babysitter can influence him.

It is the same with parents. God will hold us accountable for the job we do because He has given us the ability to do the job. Ephesians 6:4 says,
"And you fathers, do not provoke your children to wrath, but bring them up in the training and admonition of the Lord."

Colossians 3:21 states,
"Fathers, do not provoke your children lest they become discouraged."

Proverbs 29:15 offers,
"The rod and rebuke give wisdom, But a child left to himself brings shame to his mother."

Not only do these passages show that parents act while children react, they also emphasize the influence a parent possesses. Children are not to be left to raise themselves. Fathers are not to be overbearing because of the reaction it can encourage. Notice also the parent is being instructed by

God to make a choice. It seems we have overlooked the fact that if we can influence our child to become angry or discouraged, we can also influence him to be kind and positive.

The fourth reason the parent has the advantage is because God has called on the child to obey. Ephesians 6:1 states,

> "Children, obey your parents in the Lord, for this is right. 'Honor your father and mother,' which is the first commandment with promise: 'that it may be well with you and you may live long on the earth."

Several proverbs also underscore the child's call to obedience:

> "My son, hear the instruction of your father, and do not forsake the law of your mother;" (Prov. 1:8)

> "Hear, my children, the instruction of a father, And give attention to know understanding;" (Prov. 4:1)

> "My son, keep your father's command, and do not forsake the law of your mother." (Prov. 6:20)

> "A wise son heeds his father's instruction, but a scoffer does not listen to rebuke." (Prov. 13:1)

You, as a parent, have a decided advantage over your child. You are smarter. You can choose to act while they mostly react. Also, **God has given you an innate ability to parent and will hold you accountable for your stewardship of that gift.** Your child is also designed by God for obedience to you. All of this comes together under the most basic struggle you have with your child. You are to search out and know better than your child what he needs. Your child is constantly throwing out what he wants. If you do not believe you have the advantage, then you will defer to the wants of your child and make him one of those who is "left to himself." You may even wind up obeying your child instead of teaching him to obey and honor you. Of course, the respect for you he learns will translate into respect for other authorities in his life. Obeying a boss or an officer of the law is no problem when your child has first learned to obey the parent or parents God gave him.

If you grow in wisdom and discern what your child needs, then you may see Proverbs 23:24 in your life.

"The father of the righteous will greatly rejoice,
And he who begets a wise child will delight in
him."

2. Behaviors Are Not Removed So Much as Replaced

This is the second part of the Common Sense Secret and a principle all effective parents follow whether they realize it or not. Unfortunately, as the lessons of parenting have not been passed on, many of us in these days wrongly believe the aim is merely to stop a bad behavior. In effect, we are saying to the child, "Quit doing that!" No matter how hard he tries, however, he will not quit doing something by just attempting to quit. Simply put, attempting to quit something focuses us even more on doing it. As an example, try for a moment not to think of a moonlit lake with the light broken by the ripples of a warm breeze. Now, try hard not to think of the warm smells that go with the woods that surround this lake, or the gentle lapping of the waves against the rocky shore.

What happened when you tried not to think of the scene? Naturally, you thought of it, and thought of it vividly. Trying not to think of something forces us to focus on it. On the other hand, had you tried to think of something besides the scene, you would have been successful. If you think of a pink hippopotamus or a banana split the size of a tugboat, then you are not thinking of the moonlit lake. Have you forgotten this part of the Common Sense Secret?

One of the common problems I see in counseling is the issue of sibling rivalry. Usually, in some form or another, the parent is asking, "How can I get Child A to quit aggravating Child B?" In other words, rivalries tend towards "angels and devils." One child generally is nice and kind, while the other one agitates and stirs up. Besides the fact you are probably missing how your "angel" is encouraging your "devil" to agitate, there is a more basic problem. The goal cannot be simply to remove the bad behavior. Instead, you must think in terms of replacing the behavior. One child can leave another child alone by being asleep, being at someone else's house, or being tied and muzzled. None of which should be the true goal. The better option is for Child B to learn to treat Child A with kindness and love. The real goal, of course, is to have the children play well together. When children play well together, then they are not involved with sibling rivalry.

Let's take another example. About the time each of our children can pull up next to furniture, Joanna and I teach them not to touch certain items we designate as "off limits." Probably one of the rudest and least "common sense" practices of parents is to force people to remove all of their breakables when our children come over to play. We, instead, have focused on providing items for the children to play with while instructing them about items that are off limits. Realizing that behaviors are replaced, however, I created another option for our children; *the Wave*. I told our little ones they could not touch an item, but they could wave at it. One time Joanna placed a flower in a pot, which naturally drew the attention of Laura. We can't have children ripping plants out of pots, nor can we place large planters "out of reach." I firmly told Laura the plant was a "No," but that she could wave at it. She stood there and waved because she had a behavior to focus on. Another time, in a local retail store, I had given this same instruction for a stack of sale items near the floor. My son, Tripp, as a toddler dutifully waved at the items and did not touch them. Shortly, a crowd gathered, somewhat amazed, and asked, "How did you teach him to do that?" Very simply, I understand that generally behaviors are not removed, but replaced.

What behaviors have you been trying to get your child to "stop doing," but never showed them another appropriate behavior to replace it? Do you tell them to quit yelling indoors without teaching them how to talk softly? Do you tell them not to grab toys from others without teaching them how to ask politely? Do you demand from your older child to "not argue with you," but fail to give him a proper way to sit down and reason together over a concern? Why not make a quick inventory of the major struggles you have with your child? Ask yourself if you have been trying to remove a behavior without offering a new and better one to take its place.

Let's quickly review. So far, we've seen that the Common Sense Secret centers on learning to think like common sense parents think before we do what common sense parents do. Additionally, this secret is found in two important beliefs: the parent has the advantage over the child, and behaviors are not removed so much as they are replaced.

3. All Behaviors Have Their Reasons

The final part of the Common Sense Secret is probably the most life transforming. Also, if you neglect it or fail to embrace it, you'll probably never see the results you want. Can you see what the fisherman, the snake, and a bottle of bourbon teaches?

A man went fishing one day. He looked over the side of his boat and saw a snake with a frog in its mouth. Feeling sorry for the frog, he reached down, gently took the frog from the snake, and set the frog free. But then he felt sorry for the snake. He looked around the boat, but he had no food. All he had was a bottle of bourbon. So he opened the bottle and gave the snake a few shots. The snake went off happy, the frog was happy, and the man was happy to have performed such good deeds. He thought everything was great until about ten minutes passed and he heard something knock against the side of the boat. With stunned disbelief, the fisherman looked down and saw the snake was back with two frogs![3]

This principle or truism has been known throughout the ages, and has taken many different forms in the conversation and history of mankind. It is a part of your everyday life. It applies at work, in the home, at school, in science and medicine, and virtually everywhere in this world. It is a basic way to describe "the law of cause and effect." When we talk of cause and effect, we simply mean there is a reason for everything that happens. Even random and unusual things happen for a reason. Whether you believe in God or natural laws, you can still see that every event is started by another event preceding it.

Since we are looking at becoming effective parents, let's understand it in parenting terms. Whenever your child has a behavior that you do not like, or is inappropriate, then you may safely assume that there is a reason that behavior is happening. Unfortunately, most of us, before we develop our common sense in this area, haphazardly guess at the cause of our child's behavior. If you defer to experts, then your "favorite" expert will help you guess at the cause. If your expert believes that all problems are physiological, then your child's behavioral problem must be a physical problem, such as food allergies, or ADD, or hormonal imbalances, etc. We are not addressing the possible legitimacy of these causes in this section, but rather we are trying to understand a secret that will allow us to find the true cause of our child's behavior.

The third part of the Common Sense Secret is a broad principle that applies to both good and bad behavior. It also applies to your marriage, your time management, your work, and even your finances. Michael LeBoeuf calls this principle the "greatest management principle" and uses it as a foundation for businesses to receive maximum output from their employees. He states it in this form: "The things that get rewarded get done."[4] His idea is that if a business will properly reward certain behaviors, then that business will most definitely see those behaviors occur. B.F. Skinner, the famous behaviorist, both applied and misapplied this principle in seeing it as the principle that essentially governed the world.

The more folksy rendition of this principle is the idea of the "carrot and the stick." In motivating people, or animals, it is effective to use a "carrot" to attract them to move forward. The "stick" prevents them from moving backwards. The principle has also been referred to as the "pain-pleasure principle." This principle observes that human beings rapidly try to move away from pain. Next it asserts we also try to move toward pleasure or things we find enjoyable.

Another attempt to describe this principle is known as the "law of expectation" or the "Pygmalion effect." George Bernard Shaw's play *Pygmalion* illustrates how the expectations we have of others can change them. Liza Doolittle became a "proper" lady through the tutoring and encouragement of Professor Higgins.[5] This Pygmalion effect has also been documented many times, most famously through education when a teacher is told she has an "exceptional" and gifted class of students. Although the students are an average collection, the teacher's expectations and efforts result in an academically superior class. They are motivated, energized, and quick to learn; more so than any of the teacher's previous classes.

The Bible, itself, states this principle in what we call the "laws of the harvest." The principle is, *"whatever a man sows, that he will also reap"* (Gal. 6:7). The idea biblically is that God has put in place laws to govern the world, one of which is the law of sowing and reaping. When one sows to debt, he will reap debt. When one sows to friendships, he will reap friendships. When one sows to the spiritual part of his life, he will reap spiritual growth. More negatively, when one sows to evil, he will go on to worse evil. Consider two examples of this "reward principle."

First, think about the mundane world of taxes. I have no political agenda here and am very willing to pay my taxes, but the tax structure is a great example. We have a progressive income tax structure in America. Progressive means the more an individual makes the higher the applied tax rate. The idea behind this so many decades ago was that all people have to pay for the same "basic" items such as food, electricity, etc. Because this is true, it is also true that the "better off" have more disposable income after the basics are bought than do the "lesser off." The progressive tax then is focused on letting the better off shoulder a greater but "fairer" part of the tax burden.

What is the net result of this tax plan? Among other things some of us have turned down raises or income opportunities because to accept them would put us into a "higher tax bracket," thereby leaving us with less disposable income than before we got our "raise." This system, while attempting a more "equitable" taxing structure, serves to discourage the capitalistic basis of our free enterprise system. Much the same frustration was behind the famous "Boston Tea Party".

The progressive tax also encourages, or rewards, the better off to seek out loopholes and deductions to pay less.

Another proposition is the "flat tax." The flat tax simply means that everyone is taxed at the same rate, say 15%. Of course, this structure does proportionally "punish" the lesser off, as mentioned above. However, the flat tax will do something else; it will encourage everyone to make more money through hard work and wise investments. Essentially, under a flat tax, the more you make the more you keep. If people can keep more, then they tend to work to make more. If we follow the principle "what gets rewarded gets done," then we can see the flat tax "rewarding" two things. First it rewards, or encourages investments and entrepreneurship. Second, it rewards all to pay their taxes because it is simple, easy to catch cheaters with, and easy to perceive as "fair" by most of us. A final observation is that a flat tax will also "reward" simplicity in government, because a large tax bureaucracy will be totally unnecessary to collect taxes.

Now consider our principle with a parenting example. Some time ago, Joanna and I had friends over for the evening. At one point, the visiting mom needed to feed her one-year-old child. It is important to understand that this mother enjoys conversation and relishes the opportunity to visit with "adults." She continued talking while opening a jar of baby food for her youngster. As she opened the jar and introduced the spoon to her baby, the child began to scream. This went on for a while. Every spoonful was separated by a scream. Finally, the mother turned to me and said, "I just don't understand, she screams the whole time I'm feeding her." Naturally, it was easy enough to realize what was going on with "you reap as you sow" firmly planted in my own mind.

This mother was so busy in conversation or some other activity that the child didn't get to eat until she "screamed" for it. It is a simple picture, the baby screams and the mother puts food in the child's mouth. The baby chews the food and swallows it. The mother, all the while conversing, waits for the baby to scream again for more food. In effect, this mother had inadvertently taught her baby to "scream for her supper," while Dad innocently looked on. Your parenting challenges may seem bigger, but are they any different?

If you want truly to understand how profound and scriptural this principle is, read through the book of Proverbs. It shows that whatever happens is encouraged to happen. My favorite proverb for this principle is Proverbs 29:12.

"If a ruler pays attention to lies, all his servants become wicked."

In other words, if a ruler only listens to lies, it encourages his servants to lie. Once lying begins, wickedness grows out of control. What gets rewarded gets done. We reap as we sow. For every result (wicked servants), there is a cause (a ruler who listens to lies). This not only applies to kingdoms, but to families as well. If a mother pays attention to whining, all of her children become pains in the ear. If a father pays attention to sibling rivalry, all of his children will become antagonists. This principle applies to the whole of parenting, and to the good and bad behaviors we see in our children.

There is a different and easier way to say and understand this reward principle. It forms two particular tools that we can use as parents. The first is a tool for *diagnosis*, the second is a tool for *change*. In diagnosis, we want to know what the real problem is. In change, we want to encourage a new behavior to replace an undesired one.

A TOOL FOR DIAGNOSIS: *si? => ie!*

Our simple formula for diagnosing our child's "problems" is

si? => ie!

It stands for **See It? It's Encouraged!** In other words, if you see a behavior, then you may safely assume that it is somehow being encouraged. If you see a child who constantly whines or has temper tantrums, then you may safely assume that somehow the whining is being encouraged. Now, this formula does not tell us how the behavior is being encouraged, but it helps us begin to look for the real cause of the behavior. Instead of simply assuming the child is tired or needs to eat, we can use si? => ie! to begin looking at the many ways, over time, a behavior is encouraged. What is your child doing? It doesn't matter if they are good behaviors or bad ones to appreciate this tool. Take a behavior or two and watch your child through the si? => ie! formula. If you see a behavior, it's being encouraged somehow. You can count on it. It may be physiology. It may be personality. More likely, however, it is something you and others are encouraging the child to do. It is a hard but necessary fact for a common sense parent to swallow.

Realize also that the issue is not what you think encourages or discourages a particular behavior. Instead, it is a matter of how your child sees it. As the younger brother to a teenager, I followed the path of most siblings. I often irritated my brother and his friends to the point that they would mistreat me. Finally, they would throw me out of the room and ban me to the outer darkness of rejection. Why would I continue to come back for such mistreatment? It's simple. Human beings would rather be noticed and rejected than simply ignored. As in my case with my older brother, I wanted to be noticed instead of ignored. You might not see getting picked on by teenagers as a "reward," but I certainly did at that age. **The encouragement for our behaviors is often in the eye of the beholder. It is important, therefore, to look at things from your child's point of view as you apply the tool of si? => ie!**

A Tool For Change: ei! => si!

The tool for change, as we apply the Common Sense Secret, is probably the most important aspect of common sense parenting to understand and apply. The formula is simply

ei! => si!

It stands for **Encourage It! See It!** In other words, if you will begin to focus on what behaviors you want to see by concentrating your energy and efforts on encouraging them, they will happen. If you encourage a behavior, then you will see the behavior. I know I must hurriedly add that there are exceptions, which we will discuss later. However, before you dismiss this principle, just try it.

If it is helpful, think of the principle in this way: you, as a parent, are helping your child change without your child's help—you are changing your child; your child is not changing himself. The way you will do this is by making the desired behavior the equivalent of swimming downstream. You will also begin to make the undesired behavior equivalent to swimming upstream. If you've had any experience swimming, then you know it is easier to swim downstream and harder to swim upstream. The behaviors you see in your child are most probably the result of the way you and your child's environment have created a downstream effect. Your child sees his behaviors as the easiest and most rewarding. He, therefore, keeps doing the same things because it is like swimming downstream. The common sense parent knows how to change the direction of the stream! The common sense parent knows how to make it easier to do a new behavior than to keep with an old one. The common sense parent knows how to help his child change without his child's help.

A wonderful example comes from a family I helped think through these principles as they applied to their eleven-year-old son. While I was visiting, Dad made a request of his son, but received only a "yeah" as his eleven-year-old walked on down the hall. I pointed out to this Dad that he might want to "run that play until he gets it right," meaning that my tendency is to have a child come back and redo the conversation with a little more respect. As this Dad began to apply this principle over the next week, he saw a significant change in how his son used respectful language. In other words, **Encourage It! See It!** This Dad created another change in the stream as he began to apply these principles. In particular, this child had a bad habit of leaving his clothes on the floor. Mom warned him, and then Dad warned him that the next time clothes were found on his floor, the son would have to take off his present clothes and put on the old dirty ones to wear for the rest of the day. The son said, "Naw, Dad...you wouldn't do that." Sure enough Dad did do it, and not surprisingly the clothes have stayed off the floor. Now they tell me they are shifting to dealing with the towels in the bathroom. Dad's idea is that the next time he finds a towel on the bathroom floor, the son will have to shower again and dry off with the same towel before hanging it up properly. Do you think the towels will stay off the floor?

It may seem simple, but don't miss how profound this piece of common sense is. If you want to see a behavior, it must be encouraged. If you see behaviors in your child that you do not like, they are being encouraged from your child's viewpoint. Most importantly, you must apply this principle in your own unique parenting way to your own special and unique child. Don't look for ideas in other books and talk shows first. Take the principle and begin to look for ideas from your own heart and your own mind for your own home.

There is one thing, however, that I can offer that will help you in the process of designing your own ways to help your child change. All it takes is answering four "magic" questions.

5

The Four Magic Common Sense Questions

Magic is intriguing. Whether it is the illusionist who awes us by making people "float" in mid-air and objects appear from "nowhere," or the possibility of changing a frog into a prince with a kiss; people love magic.

Of course, in the Christian tradition we have been leary of magic. The battle between Moses and Pharaoh's sorcerers, the bizarre and magical pagan religions surrounding Israel, and the burning of magic books in Acts 19:19, add up to a strong case against magic. To use the word "magic" in a chapter title is intriguing, but dangerous. Intriguing because we, as parents, would love to have a few magic questions we could use as a spell to change the destiny of our child.

Dangerous because too much faith in a technique or human notion can undermine the role of God in our lives.

If in parenting, you have hoped for this kind of magic over your child, then you will not find it here. There is a kind of magic though, for us as parents, in the wisdom of asking and answering four strategic questions.

Magic, in our sense, is not occultic or dangerous, but something that seems to have a supernatural effect because of the dramatic results it brings. It is not false to say that these questions are magic. Indeed, if you will give an honest effort to use them, along with the new understanding you've gained so far, you will be surprised at how dramatically and quickly your child can change.

One word of warning, however. As you begin to see just how capable you are of influencing your child's behavior, don't think you can perfectly control all of your child's actions. The very thing we have stressed all along is that you definitely can influence your child. This ability, however, is something to steward well as a parent before God, not something to abuse.

A Short Review

We need to recall what we learned about the value of questions in Chapter 4. Questions are vital to help us think clearly about solutions. In fact, if you are not yet a common sense parent, then the belief you hold and the questions you ask are the major hurdles for you. If you haven't quite embraced this idea, then re-read Chapters 3 and 4, marking with a colored pen everything that strikes you.

Two quotes from Chapter 3 are worth repeating: "The difference between common sense parents and the rest is found largely in the questions they ask," and "Right solutions follow right questions."

The value of these questions is that they will help you

understand what is happening with your child, and what you can do to encourage change. If you are not seeing the things in your child that you would like to see, then it is almost guaranteed that you are not asking the right questions.

These Four Magic Questions are really just a starter kit that I have found to be helpful and common among effective parents. As you grow in your own common sense, you will add a few magic questions of your own.

THE FOUR MAGIC QUESTIONS

1. *What do I see?*
2. *What do I want to see?*
3. *How is what I see being encouraged?*
4. *How can I encourage what I want to see, and discourage everything else?*

These Four Magic Questions follow from our two formulas: si? => ie! (See It? It's Encouraged!) and ei! => si! (Encourage It! See It!). These questions will help you understand and use these formulas.

The four questions walk you through a process of thinking through your child's behavior from the problem to the solution, and they occur in a particular order. Moreover, there are two ways to apply these questions. First, you can apply them to your child's entire life and behaviors. Second, you can apply them to any specific problem or challenge.

Let's briefly consider the aim of each of these questions.

1. What Do I See?

This question is often the most difficult for many of us. It helps us to be objective instead of interpreting what is happening through our emotions or assumptions. For example, what do you see when you see a small child on the ground crying? Some of you see a hurt child, while others see a child crying for attention or for Mommy to pick him up. The only objective answer is that you see a child lying on the ground crying.

Instead of trying to at first figure out why something is happening, we need to simply focus on what is happening. Consider a few more examples.

Opinion: *What Do I Assume?*	Observation: *What Do I See?*"
"My child is arguing with me and showing me disrespect."	"My child is answering my every request with a question."
"My child is growing away from the family."	"My child is hanging around friends I don't think are a good influence on him."
"My child is undisciplined."	"My child is not turning in completed homework according to his teacher."
"My child is shy."	"My child hides behind me when meeting someone new."

There is a great need for us as parents to develop this skill of observation, because most of us are very unpracticed at just seeing the facts. We tend to rush to interpret them, often mistaking what is happening. With a mistake in the facts, what hope do we really have to solve the situation? Learn to simply and accurately ask and answer "What do I see?"

2. What Do I Want to See?

The power behind this question is that it gets us to develop a vision for our child's actions and life. It also moves us away from merely reacting to our children. In the middle of hurried lives and waning energy, most of us tend to "wait" for things to happen. Waiting on your child, though, only lets him run your home and ruin his life: "...*But a child left to himself brings shame to his mother.*" (Prov. 29:15b).

We don't (or shouldn't) wait for our car to break; we keep it on a maintenance schedule. We don't (or shouldn't) wait for a job to come our way; we apply for it. The list goes on. We are to lead and develop our children, which requires some idea or vision of where to go. Certainly we should discover and encourage the development of their own gifts and not our "dreams" for them. Dad who never got to play football, or Mom who never was a beauty pageant winner, should not try to live his or her dreams through the children. However, having a vision for their character and morals is exactly what Dad and Mom should "dream" about.

By asking, "What do I want to see?," we can begin to focus on those things to develop in our child's life. We also get a clear picture of what desired behavior needs to replace the undesired one. Consider our examples again.

What Do I See?	What Do I Want to See?
"My child is answering my every request with a question."	"I want to see my child obey me or commit to obey me before asking any questions."
"My child is hanging around friends I don't think are a good influence on him."	"I want to see my child keeping company with friends who are a good influence on him."
"My child is not turning in completed homework according to his teacher."	"I want to see my child turn his completed homework in on time, and have his teacher surprise me with a note about the change."
"My child hides behind me when meeting someone new."	"I want to see my child stand at my side and politely say, 'Hello, I'm _____; it's nice to meet you.'"

There are no limits and no set of directions to this strategic question. There are many good books and resources for determining what kinds of behaviors you can expect from your children (see the Selected Bibliography at the end of this book). My goal is not to tell you what your standards should be, but to challenge you to lead your child by setting in your mind and heart the behaviors and actions you want to encourage in your child. The best of all resources, of course, is the Bible.

A final warning must be added as you work with this question. Please don't limit your dreams to what you think is possible. Thinking, "But my child would never do that" only kills the power of Question 2. Answer it as though failure is impossible.

3. How Is What I See Being Encouraged?

The third of our Magic Questions takes us back to Question 1, but it goes a step further. This question helps us understand the behavior or actions we observe. Often it is difficult to see exactly how something is being encouraged, so don't give up. If you persist you will unravel the mystery of your child's behavior.

We are clearly assuming here that our principle of si? => ie! is true. If we see a behavior, then something is encouraging it. There may be exceptions, but they are rare. Let's re-visit our examples and fill in possible answers to Question 3.

What Do I See?	How Is What I See Being Encouraged?
"My child is answering my every request with a question."	"My child is extremely curious and simply wants to learn." OR "I'm answering his question before he obeys, so I'm encouraging him to delay obedience by engaging in conversations with him."

"My child is hanging around friends I don't think are a good influence on him."	"My child is getting more encouragement and support from his friends than from his family. Maybe they listen more while I lecture more? Maybe they hang out and I'm just in a hurry?"
"My child is not turning in completed homework according to his teacher."	"The teacher did not inform us of the problem for six weeks; therefore my child was getting away with it. Also, we have not been checking his homework each night before bed."
"My child hides behind me when meeting someone new."	"When my husband pointed out that I always apologize by saying, 'she's our shy one,' I realized I've probably encouraged her to live up to that label."

These are just examples and there could be other reasons why these behaviors have been encouraged. The point is for you to begin to look for the cause behind the action. Answering Question 3 properly gives a great foundation to help your child change without your child's help.

4. How Can I Encourage What I Want to See and Discourage Everything Else?

This question is the most magical of our questions. This question begins to set in motion the innate gift of God within parents. It moves us to become our own experts for our own child.

Question 4 requires something you may not be very skilled at yet, brainstorming. The key is to simply get as many ideas as possible without criticizing or throwing away any of them. If the idea is related to the action, then all the better.

70 / THE ABSOLUTE QUICKEST WAY...

However, anything that encourages your child will work. As you study your child, you will begin to figure out how to answer Question 4, and continue to build a list of ways to encourage your child. Of course, the shortcut is to ask your child what he thinks will encourage him. You'll be surprised when he starts to give you some great ideas.

Encouragement is not the only part of this question. Discouraging other behaviors and actions is also important. A carrot is good and a stick is too, but to use both in proper proportions is a powerful combination. The things to discourage are in the answers to Question 3. Let's look at our examples again.

What Do I Want to See?	How Can I Encourage/Discourage?
"I want to see my child obey me or commit to obey me before asking any questions."	"I simply will not answer a question until after he obeys or tells me 'I'm going to do it, but may I ask a question?' Also, I'm going to tell my child that he gets $1 every time he can get me to answer a question before he obeys."
"I want to see my child keeping company with friends who are a good influence on him."	"I need to work on my friendship with him. I think I'll begin to let him pick one activity each month just for us. I could also begin to provide activities, the car, extra money, or other encouragements whenever he spends time with some of his 'good influence' friends."

"I want to see my child turn his completed homework in on time, and have his teacher surprise me with a call or note about the change in my child."

"The new rule will be Earn Fun with Homework. It will be homework first and fun second. Outside activities, friends, TV, etc., will be allowed after homework is completed. I'll also throw in a special treat when the teacher gives me that call or note!"

"I want to see my child stand at my side and politely say, 'Hello, I'm _____. It's nice to meet you.'"

"We'll just practice until we get it right—first, in private, then as we meet people. I'll explain that 'this is my polite child' (not my shy one) and praise her as she follows the plan. I'm also going to have to have a serious consequence until she obeys."

Again, these are just a few examples. Please remember, you are to become the expert for your child. You are better able to figure out what will encourage and discourage behaviors in your child than any experts, books, or magazines. Don't be afraid to gather ideas from others, but usually the best ideas for Question 4 come from your own mind and heart; no one knows your child like you, nor can they.

THE EXERCISE

The most important thing you can do now is to apply these questions. It will take some work, but as soon as possible, you and your spouse (if applicable) need to sit down and answer these questions for each child. Ideally you should both read the book, but at least sit down and work through the Four Magic Questions together.

When I say work through each question, I mean to sit and answer all of these questions at the same time, and as fully as possible for each child. More children may mean more sessions, but it will be worth it. If this is overwhelming, then start with a small win. Pick a single behavior for each child and focus the questions on it. Appendix A may be copied or used to guide you through this process. Remember, you are seeking to develop and gain wisdom. The process takes time and isn't easy for any of us. Give yourself time to learn to observe and answer these questions. This is the most strategic battle to recapture your parenting gift. If you lose here, you'll lose. But if you win; what a victory!

When you do this exercise two important things will happen. First, you will create a new way to look at your child and his actions. What is more important, you will do this together, possibly becoming like-minded about your child for the first time. You can even throw the list away if you wish, because the impact of the exercise alone will begin to transform your perspective. The second thing that will happen, if you keep the list, will be that you will have a catalog of great ideas to help your child change. Someday it may even be a great gift to give your grown children as they begin families of their own.

I hope this is starting to make sense. If it's not, then you probably just need a few examples...

6

Examples!
Examples! Examples!

It was a great idea, so they thought. Fort Worth wanted to get people to read more so a local radio station decided to put money inside random books at a major library. The result? Thousands of books were opened and thrown to the floor by the determined hoard of people. What happened?

Our focus throughout has been to understand a very basic principle of human nature. We've stated it as **ei!** => **si!** (Encourage It! See It!). We have also looked at this principle in a form to diagnose problems, stated **si?** => **ie!** (See It? It's Encouraged!). If we apply this principle to the library scene, we can quickly understand what went wrong. What do we see? Thousands of books on the floor as people frantically look for money inside the books. How was what we see encouraged? People like free money. Money is inside books. The faster one looks, the more money one finds. It is quite simple. The radio station set up a perfect system to throw books on the floor, not to have them read! If you see it, it's encouraged.

In your own child-rearing practices, do you sometimes set up the same kind of silly plan that rewards the wrong thing? Do you then follow one mistake with another one by blaming your child? Should we blame the people for throwing the books on the floor? Perhaps. It certainly isn't respectful of property. But they aren't the first ones to be blamed. They were reacting to the actions of the radio station. Our children also are not primarily to blame. Our children react to the actions of the parents, which, as we have learned, gives us a great advantage.

How could the radio station have approached this situation better? If it had applied two of our questions from Chapter 5 then everything would have been different. What if the station had asked, "What do we want to see?" Surely the management would have concluded that they wanted to see more people actually reading books or at least learning to use the library. They certainly would not have wanted to see thousands of books on the library floor. Obviously they didn't take the first step by getting a clear idea of the result they wanted.

Next, the radio station could have asked, "How can we encourage what we want to see (people reading) and discourage everything else?" With this question they might have originated any number of fresh ideas. Give money for book reports that are hand written. Even if they didn't read it, someone will practice writing. How about brief oral exams when a book is turned in, or a multiple choice test devised for quality works of literature? Just recently a junior high school had the satisfaction of watching the principal "kiss a pig" after the students completed an extracurricular reading plan. Perhaps seeing a mayor kiss a pig wouldn't motivate a city to actually read, but something surely would. The point is that the principle works and shows up daily in our lives.

Another example of Encourage It! See It! is in language and vocabulary. You hear "y'all" in the South quite a bit, but hardly at all in the North. Why is this? Language is learned from the people around you. When the people around you can't understand you unless you use their language, it is simple to conclude that learning "their" language is the best choice. You can't say "you guys" in Mobile, Alabama, without drawing some looks. Nor can you go to Buffalo, New York and say "y'all" and not get pegged for an outsider.

What about your child and language? Haven't you held the book away from your child until he or she says something resembling "book" or "please?" You immediately encourage that response by saying "Good girl! You said, 'Please!'" This is the same way you help your child change other behavior. When a behavior you don't like persists, it is likely that it is being encouraged. The following are a few real life examples of the principle in action.

THE FIVE MINUTE RULE AND A GOOD BOUNCE

The first two examples come from my own parenting experiences. A few years ago I invented the Five Minute Rule, which addresses a very basic problem most parents face.

You're in a store. After only a short time, your child says, "When are we going to go?" or the dreaded and grating, "I wanna go home." I realize that shopping is tough on children, but learning patience is an important life skill to learn. Imagine your child never learning patience, arriving at his first college class to ask the professor after the first twenty minutes, "Prof., when are we going to go?" That child will probably get to leave all too quickly! The Five Minute Rule simply says that every time one of my children asks me about leaving, we stay an extra five minutes. Needless to say, they catch on quickly. On one occasion Forrest, my three-year-old, not knowing the rule, asked to go home. Instantly Tripp, the oldest, cupped Forrest's mouth and said, "No Forrest, you don't understand. We'll just have to stay longer if we ask to leave." If it's encouraged, it'll happen.

My second example has to do with Tripp's cerebral palsy. Tripp, because of a lesion on his brain at birth, is mildly spastic on the right side of his body. He finally began to walk at twenty-three months, but had a great deal of difficulty. At about this time we discovered his cerebral palsy and felt all of the sorrow and fears as parents of our first baby. Nonetheless, I began to hold Joanna back every time Tripp fell down, which he did a lot. I had to hold her because, as I've learned, Mommies don't like their babies to hurt themselves. We just couldn't pick him up every time, however. I told Joanna that Tripp was going to fall a lot in his life, and if we start picking him up now he won't learn to stand on his own. Instead of running to him we learned to say, "Good bounce!" A few years later the teenage babysitters at a church function confirmed our plan. "Mrs. Lybrand," they told Joanna. "Tripp is really neat. We saw him fall on the playground, but he'd just get up and keep going. Most of the other children just fall and cry until we pick them up!" If you see it, it's encouraged.

Other Real Life Examples

- One teenage daughter has the minor, but frustrating, habit of leaving drinking glasses on a wooden dresser. The result is that stains and water rings are destroying the finish. When Dad understands and applies common sense, he decides to remove the dresser from her room.

After a few days it is returned, but with the guarantee of removal if it becomes a depository for drinking glasses. No more glasses appeared.

- A mother has the constant problem of her little angelic five-year-old leaving the kitchen with food and roaming the house while eating. No matter how much she lectures and fusses at her daughter, food is still found around the house. After applying the Four Magic Questions, the answer dawns on Mom. The next time the girl leaves the kitchen with food, Mom simply takes the food away. The timing is a little hard because the item is a candy bar, but the angel no longer eats while flying.

- A boy is promised a hunting trip with his Dad. Two weeks remain, and so do many chores. Dad makes a list of chores and assigns a value to each one...in shotgun shells. The shells are placed in a large see-through container, and as chores are not done on time, shotgun shells are removed. The son was very diligent and had plenty of shells for hunting.

- Another teenaged son is given a list of responsibilities, including getting ready for school on time each morning. Each of these expectations is clearly explained with appropriate deadlines. As these responsibilities are ignored or neglected, a large X is placed on a calendar to represent an afternoon apart from any friends or free time. He now knows just how much he can do early in the morning.

- A young son gets in the habit of arguing with Mom about anything. She finally learns to simply ignore him except when he is polite and non-argumentative. Walking out of the room a few times gets the message across.

- A Dad gets tired of hearing "Yeah" instead of "Yes Sir!" from his three young children. He offers them ten M&Ms each at the end of a two-day period. The catch is that each "yeah" gets one M&M removed. Shortly a rule is added; tattling on each other for not saying "Yes Sir!" also removes a piece of candy. Of course, in this family sweets are a treat, not a daily event. Now the habit is established, though it sounds a little like a military base around the house.

- One young girl sticks her tongue out at others, especially family members. A simple rule is established that every time she sticks her tongue out, she is not allowed to eat dinner with the rest of the family. The family is happy to see her at the dinner table, and her tongue is put to better uses now.

- An eighth-grade son has the habit of not hanging up the towel after his shower. Dad comes up with a new rule: "If it is not hung up, it will be replaced with a smaller towel." The need to dry off overcomes the need to be sloppy.

- One family has the rule that if a small portion of vegetables given at supper is not eaten within the first ten minutes, then the vegetable portion will be doubled.

- A small child has the habit of running into a room and interrupting an adult conversation. Mom and Dad decide to begin sending the child out of the room and have him come in properly, placing a hand on the parent, and waiting for permission to speak. He still runs into the room, but he doesn't interrupt.

Some other quick examples: bikes left in the driveway are put up for a twenty-four hour period, arguing over a toy gets the toy removed, bad attitudes are enjoyed alone in one's room, fight with friends while they are visiting and they get taken home, no seconds (except vegetables) of a favorite until progress is made with every food on the plate, and school papers that do not receive passing grades are rewritten until a passing grade is reached (you'll be surprised how many teachers will help you with this, and how few rewrites you'll see).

The point of these examples is not to get you to use M&Ms or other enticements but to show you a child's natural desire to please his parents. Your child is desperate for your love, encouragement, approval, and acceptance. Learning to distinguish between your child being accepted and his behavior being unacceptable is important. It is a great part of your influence to realize that, deep down, your child really wants you to support and be pleased with him. Often, when this doesn't happen, it is because your child has been encouraged to use bad behavior to get your attention. You are so important to your child that negative attention is better than none at all. What would your life be like if you encouraged your child to gain your attention and support through good behavior?

Remember the priority of balance. Most children, for example start out as little artists. They draw stick figures and odd shapes that don't look like much of anything. We parents, however, shout, "It's a Picasso!" and display it openly on the refrigerator for all to admire. What does that do for a child? It motivates him to draw another one. Oddly though, if we praise every single picture the same enthusiastic way, most children will grow disinterested in drawing or never improve much. If we can learn to honestly praise the better drawings and lovingly send the other ones back for more work, we are encouraging the best from our children. They need to know where boundaries are and what improvement looks like. They need to know when we are pleased and displeased. This is part of the learning process, just as the physical world teaches them about pain and pleasure.

All of this takes us back to the belief that your child can change and that you can help him change. The greatest challenge, however, is for you to begin learning how this works.

My experience with parents is that this chapter will leave you wanting more and more examples. Why? The principle is clear and obvious and easy to demonstrate again and again. Why do you want more examples? You want me to tell you what to do—you are still victimized by the Expert Syndrome. You haven't yet gained the confidence you need because you haven't experienced your own gift and power to parent. It is a revolution, and we need a large dose of courage to take parenting back. Ralph Waldo Emerson observed that, "The greater part of courage is having done it before." You want more examples because I haven't yet addressed your exact situation. You are still looking for an expert to tell you what to do. I refuse to do it. You must become the expert for your own child. Study that child and figure out how he ticks and how to help him make good choices that will please both you and him.

My advice is simple: First, pursue wisdom (Chapter 2), then apply the Four Magic Questions to whatever you are facing with your child (Chapter 5), and finally, let me remind you that you can do it! God would not give you children without giving you the ability to parent. It may need some developing, but you really can become an effective parent if you will begin.

Finally, there is a shortcut. It actually is the most important secret of all for a true Parenting Revolution. Your parenting and your life will never be the same if you learn...

7

The Absolute Quickest Way to Help Your Child Change

In the popular "western" movie, *Quigley Down Under*, the hero states while lost in the outback, "Don't know where I'm goin', but no use in bein' late." So it goes with our hurried lives.

Our time is valuable. Our days are full. Anything that allows us to accomplish more in less time is instantly accepted as useful. No wonder a "shortcut" is so attractive. If we can spend less energy and arrive earlier, we've beaten Time! So we think. But often, a shortcut is a gimmick at best, and a long fall, at worst.

There is a shortcut, however, to help your child change (for the better) without your child's help. It's not a parenting skill, but it is consistent with everything we've learned so far. It will also dramatically affect your child's life and behavior. You may, in fact, have skipped every chapter and opened straight to this one. If you did, you don't have to go back, but let me warn you: this principle is not for the faint of heart. This shortcut is powerful, but potentially difficult. This chapter explains the most influential power over your child's life, with the exception of God's direct work on the human heart. Without understanding the previous chapters, it will be hard to fully appreciate this ultimate shortcut. Also, combining this secret with all of the others we've looked at is the total effective parenting package. The greatest benefit will come if you stop reading here and start at the beginning.

What could it be that is so powerful over the lives of our children? Why are we just now getting to this principle so late in the discussion? What do we mean when we say it is difficult? Each of these questions and many more will come to your mind as you reflect on this shortcut to help your child change. Questions are good, debating to keep from facing facts is not. Many parents who read this chapter may find feelings of anger, hopelessness, and frustration well up from deep within. Please don't see those feelings as a reason to put this book down. Instead, be curious about your feelings. They are trying to tell you something. Learn to ask things like, "What is it in me that is so resistant to what I'm learning here?" If you can keep your objectivity as you are committed to learning, you'll find great hope. The truth really cannot hurt you, and it will help your child change!

Remember how we learned earlier that, "The only difference between a problem and a solution is that we understand the solution?" Well, we face the same issue here. There is a solution available to parents that is seldom understood and often ignored.

Consider an example. She was about three when her parents decided to stop her from sucking her thumb. It seemed easy enough to discipline her for sucking her thumb, but suddenly she began to pull her hair out in little tufts. I was invited to help solve this dilemma, and we saw some improvement quickly. We simply tried to discourage the bad behavior as we've discussed in the earlier chapters. After a short time, however, this little girl began to pull her hair out at night and carefully hide it under her pillow! We tried everything, but it just wasn't working. I personally thought we were taking a wise approach, but this little girl wasn't responding. When sound, common sense practices don't work on a three-year-old, then you can be confident that something in the family more powerful than your direct actions is encouraging the behavior.

That something is the relationship between husband and wife. **A healthy relationship between Mom and Dad is the absolute quickest way to help your child change.** But let me warn you again: though this shortcut is powerful (the most influential power over your child's life, with the exception of God's direct work), it is also potentially difficult, often ignored, and seldom understood. I'm warning you so you won't give up, not to keep you from starting.

If you're a single parent, don't think this doesn't apply to you too. You may marry again, or you may still be seeing problems in your child because of enduring relationship struggles. But, why is this such a powerful influence, even a shortcut, to help your child change? The reason is simple and follows the underlying principle in this book—"if you see it, it's encouraged." The simple fact is that healthy marriages tend to produce healthy children, and unhealthy marriages tend to produce unhealthy children. Like breeds like. That is why, even if you are attempting to encourage the right things in your child, but are not living the right things in your marriage, you'll have little success in changing your child. You actually fall victim to the very thing you never liked as a child, "Do as I say, not as I do."

If your marriage is healthy and growing, though you seldom properly discipline your child, that child will still have a better chance of turning out well than the child with parents possessing great skills but a sour marriage. **The shortcut is to focus on healing your marriage.**

How can you heal your marriage? In fact, you may not even think much is wrong with it. The following is a simple test that will help you discern the healthiness of your marriage.

1. Are you and your spouse more distant now or about the same emotionally as you were a year ago?
2. Do you or your spouse favor one child over another? (Just ask your children if you don't know!)
3. Do you or your spouse feel the need to justify to an inlaw(s) the decisions or actions made by one or both of you?
4. Is anything or anyone other than God more important to you or your spouse than each other? (Include parents, friends, children, work, church, etc.)
5. For no medical reason, do you and your spouse come together sexually less than once per week on average?
6. Do your children think that every member of the family should be loved equally, including the love between you and your spouse?

If you answer "yes" to only one of these, it indicates a potential problem in the relationship. More than one indicates even more serious problems.

The focus of this test is to look at how you as a couple see your relationship compared to the other relationships in your lives. The simple and common sense truth is that health in a marriage comes when the relationship is elevated above every other human relationship. No child, friend, or in-law, is to be placed above the marriage. Moreover, no other relationship has more potential for true intimacy and closeness than marriage.

It isn't just common sense, it is also part of God's original design for men and women. Consider the following passages from the Bible:

> *"Therefore a man shall leave his father and mother and be joined to his wife, and they shall become one flesh. And they were both naked, the man and his wife, and were not ashamed."*
> (Gen. 2:24-25)

> *"So husbands ought to love their own wives as their own bodies; he who loves his wife loves himself. For no one ever hated his own flesh, but nourishes and cherishes it, just as the Lord does the church. For we are members of His body, of His flesh and of His bones. "For this reason a man shall leave his father and mother and be joined to his wife, and the two shall become one flesh." This is a great mystery, but I speak concerning Christ and the church. Nevertheless let each one of you in particular so love his own wife as himself, and let the wife see that she respects her husband."*
> (Eph. 5:28-33)

There is a great deal we could learn here, but one thing is preeminent. The husband and wife relationship is to be special, separate, and unique to other relationships. It is to be intimate, loving, and respectful. It is to be "a circle of two" that neither encourages nor permits any other relationship to compete with it. I believe, and many researchers and thinkers (experts) agree, that the greatest damaging influence on children is the failure of a marriage to maintain this standard. Further, the problems we see are largely encouraged by violating this God-invented, unique relationship.

Specifically, the phrase "leave father and mother and be joined" underscores the uniqueness and priority of marriage. First, leaving father and mother to be joined together elevates marriage above parental affiliations. Secondly, since our children someday will leave to be married, our relationship with them must come after our own marriage. It is the simple and clear design of God that marriage is to be placed above all other relationships. Even common sense befriends us here. What husband truly wants his wife to be emotionally closer to another person than she is to him? What wife wants her husband to be closer to a friend or his mother than he is to her? We are only emphasizing here what you know is true in your heart. Marriage is to be the unique and special human relationship above all others, and only the most cynical or hopeless would doubt it.

Why is understanding marriage as a priority so important? It is important because accepting the truth about marriage is a powerful beginning toward healing any marriage, and a healthy marriage encourages the growth of healthy children. The simple fact is that the relationship between Dad and Mom is so powerful that few children overcome its influence.

If you understand our main principle, "if you see it, it's encouraged," then you can understand what happens in the family. Each child has some very basic needs. He needs to feel safe. He needs to feel valued or significant. Safety and significance, however, must be balanced. No child feels as safe as when he is loved by a Mom and Dad who love each other. And, believe it or not, no child feels as significant as when his parents are most significant to one another. The sense of safety and significance directly flows from the relationship between the parents. When you and your spouse's relationship is stuck in the mud, what chance do effective parenting techniques really have? Your child simply gets caught in the middle, using his behavior to try to communicate with you. In his own way, your child could be trying to fix the relationship. He could be trying to get you both to act like a team by concentrating on him. He could be screaming about his own pain because of the screaming already occurring between the two of you.

Let's prove this point with your own experience. Think back over your own childhood. How close were your parents? Was it deep or superficial? Where they in turmoil? Was their conflict open, or hidden? Do you remember how you felt the first time you wondered if your parents might get a divorce? Do you remember how it scared you, how you prayed in your own way that things would be OK?

You see, in your own childhood you knew intuitively that their relationship was profoundly important to you. If you only have memories of your parents' closeness, then be thankful and responsible to pass along such a wonderful heritage to your children. Common sense and the Scriptures both affirm that a healthy marriage is the shortcut to healthy children.

"But," you ask, "aren't there times when breaking up for the sake of the children is the best thing for them? You know, when there are irreconcilable differences. Keeping the marriage together only causes more pain and suffering for the children, leading to greater behavioral problems."

The idea of "breaking up for the kids" is a very old and very wrong idea. First, it would be worth your effort to read a *Reader's Digest* article titled, "Divorce and Kids: The Evidence Is In." In the article, Barbara Dafoe Whitehead documents the politically incorrect, but overwhelming, evidence concerning the effects of divorce on children.[6]

Second, and more important, the argument justifying divorce for the kids is actually an argument that doesn't think of the kids at all. What you are really doing is trying to justify quitting. Think about it. If you are really thinking about what's best for the children, then the option is clear: Improve the marriage! If you really love your children, do them the biggest favor of all, love your spouse. Work on the marriage. It is the sure-fire quickest way to help their behavior change. It is also the most fail-safe option.

Some statistics suggest that one-half to two-thirds of all marriages in the United States end in divorce. It is a painful tragedy and never should be handled lightly in any discussion. For a moment, though, consider the repercussions of a divorce. In an average situation where divorce occurs, both spouses could remarry. With a remarriage you suddenly have a set of complications. Each of the marriages may bring other children into the family whom you and your children will have to learn to love. You may barely get to know these new children, and your own children have to figure out how to get along with their new siblings. Naturally, your children and the new children bring all of their behavioral problems together. Does your spouse pay child support? What if a payment or two is missed? Your new spouse begins to resent having to pay for your deadbeat spouse's neglect. On the other hand, it may be that your new spouse resents some of your income going to "that other person" who probably isn't spending the money properly on the children. Meanwhile, you can't fully enjoy your new relationship as you had hoped, because in the back of your mind you know that your new spouse has taken the kids and left before. You can't really be a parent to your new children because you and your new spouse can't fully be a team. After all, they are your spouse's children. If you don't cooperate, they might leave. Your new spouse has made a decision, "nothing is coming between my children and me. They're the most important thing in my life." This means that you will always be second to the children. What hope does that marriage have for intimacy? Worse still, all of this is further multiplied and complicated by the fact that there are still two more sets of families involved because of the new spouses' own previous divorces. And couples actually think it will be better for all parties involved if they get divorced.

If you think all of this sounds confusing, you're right. If you think it couldn't happen to you, you're dead wrong. With few exceptions, seeking to heal the marriage you are in requires the least pain and least effort, with the most promising results.

How To Heal Your Marriage

Many parents who read this chapter may feel angry, hopeless, and frustrated. Don't run away from those feelings, and don't let them stop you from continuing to read. Instead, be curious about your feelings. They are trying to tell you something. Many paths lead to a healthy marriage, but in our desperate days there are three crucial ingredients.

1. Quit Focusing on "Trying Not to Divorce"

While this may seem inconsequential, it is probably the most basic safeguard in any marriage. In order for a marriage to break up, a concerted effort to "save" the relationship must have occurred. There are several important reasons this effort to save must happen in any break up. First, love or commitment of any kind insists that a couple can't merely "quit" without a cause. In every relationship, getting to the level of marriage necessarily involves a series of wonderful moments and experiences that become the foundation for the greatest ingredient of a growing relationship: hope. The couple hopes for what the relationship can become together;

in a sense, they are drawn together and toward the future with this hope in mind.

The first sign of problems in a marriage is seldom reason enough to quit since there is a reserve of hope available. Relationships end when they are seen as hopeless. It is at the crucial juncture of admitting the relationship has problems that most couples make a fatal and very un-common sense decision. They decide to "try to keep the marriage from falling apart." The decision is fatal. It will only lead to the final collapse of the marriage. If you have made this decision, please decide right this moment to turn from it. Commit to never consider it in any relationship for the rest of your life.

The second reason couples start working at "trying not to divorce" is guilt. Breaking up is a process of blame. The battle is between two former friends who are seeking to have the opponent carry away all the guilt for the failure of the marriage. Sometimes the relationship has drifted so far apart that there is a "no fault" attitude. As the song goes, "There ain't no good guy, there ain't no bad guy, there's only you and me, and we just disagree." Songs and exceptions not with-standing, most divorces have guilty and bitter people seeking to place all of the fault on one or the other.

A third reason for the attempt to not break up is the need for a reason to divorce. Couples really can't move instantly from being in love and committed to ending the relationship. There must be a reason to end it. Working at not splitting up will help you find a reason by beginning a cycle of painful experiences that eventually out number the pleasurable ones. At this point a couple gets permission to end it. "We tried. It's just too painful. It won't work." And so it won't.

The fourth reason is the most important one. The issue is focus. Whenever a couple begins to focus on not ending the relationship, they have turned their focus on the very thing they wish to avoid. I illustrated this point in Chapter 4 when I told you not to think about a moonlit lake, softly rippling in a warm breeze. Any effort to "not" do something leads us to inadvertently focus on what we are wanting to avoid. Try an experiment right now: Get a watch or timer and try not to swallow for 15 seconds. Really focus on not swallowing.

Unless you cheated by focusing on something else, you began to experience an overwhelming need to swallow. Indeed, you were probably more conscious and thankful to get to swallow than you've experienced in a long, long, time. It is really simple. We become as we focus. A person who focuses on the negatives of the past becomes depressed. One who focuses on the possible negatives of the future becomes anxious. A person who vows to never be like Dad or Mom becomes just like them.

So what happens when a couple focuses on "trying not to divorce?" Divorce! If you want your marriage to improve, no matter how good or bad it is right now, change your focus. Refuse to use the divorce word. Turn from "trying not to" to "trying to." Make your focus improving the marriage. **Commit to see how close two people can get before they die.** Use questions like, "Are we closer now than six months ago?" or "What could we do together to make our love grow?"

The more you focus on improving the marriage, the further you get from even the possibility of divorce. At their fiftieth anniversary, I asked my grandfather how he and my grandmother lasted fifty years. "It's simple," he said. "We married for keeps." It really is simple. Every marriage experiences tough times and struggles. Successful marriages, however, focus on growing together and learn to see the struggles as stages of growth. It all begins with a decision and a constant focus: How close can you and your spouse get in this one lifetime you've been given? Ask each other, "Are you willing to find out with me?"

2. Apply the Four Magic Questions to Your Marriage.

Remember the questions to apply to your child? They work for your marriage too. Try sitting down after a good meal in a nice restaurant and walk through these questions for your marriage or any areas of struggle (for example, finances, communication, making love, recreation, fixing up the house, laughing more together, dates, etc.). You may be shocked, if not a little embarrassed, that you both have created your struggles by encouraging the wrong things in your relationship. Ask, "In our marriage . . ."

1. What do we see?
2. What do we want to see?
3. How is what we see being encouraged?
4. How can we encourage what we want to see and discourage everything else?

If your spouse won't participate (don't guess, ask), then go through these questions by yourself. If you will apply them in the first person, then you will discover many ways to help your spouse change without your spouse's help.

3. Find a Supportive Environment.

What are the people you spend time with like? Are they making their marriages work? How do their children behave? Isn't it curious that you like your children to spend time with a good influence but you don't do the same for yourself? Whether we like it or not, the fact is that we will become like the people we're around the most. This may be the hardest step to follow, but you must find relationships that are successful in the areas where you are lacking. To put it another way, you'll never be like the people you don't hang around. You don't have to give up your friends as much as you need to add some new ones. Just as in sports, you'll never improve your game if you only play against those who are only as good as you are. Playing against better players encourages you to stretch. Spending time with people who are making marriage and parenting work will do the same.

So where do you find these people? The best bet is church. The church is still the singlemost pro-marriage and pro-family organization around. If you don't like church it probably isn't church as much as it is a bad past experience. All churches are not the same. Just as there are a great variety of restaurants in America, there are also a great variety of churches. It isn't a "shopping expedition," but if you'll keep searching you will find a place to reinforce and promote all you hope for your marriage and children.

In our church over the past ten years, we have only seen two or three divorces. We don't mean that divorced people don't attend, they certainly do. Nor do we mean that no one has ever left the church and gotten divorced. We mean that of those who have stayed and really sought to belong, we have seen most struggling marriages healed and transformed. We are focused on making marriages and families work, therefore we all work together to encourage one another. In fact, we have a saying for newcomers: You're welcome to bring your problems, you're just not welcome to leave them unsolved!

When you look for a church, find out if it is growing and offers help for marriage and parenting. A growing church with these priorities is likely the right environment. Also, and this should not surprise you, find out if it believes and teaches the timeless Word of God. Sadly, many churches really do not; it's a gem in the rough when you find a church faithful to the Scriptures. You will find that when you are teachable and well taught, you will change forever.

A WORD TO SINGLE PARENTS

All of this discussion may have seemed irrelevant to you if you are a single parent with no prospect (or perhaps no interest) in a future marriage. How does all of this apply? First, realize that you have a challenge. One of the worst mistakes most of us make is to ignore the seriousness of serious situations. Second, don't despair. Most of what you've read can be applied. Specifically, you need to begin working toward an emotional reconciliation with your spouse. It is still deep within your child for his parents to "get along," even if they are divorced. Never mind if the other parent won't cooperate at first, follow the advice from Romans:

> *"Repay no one evil for evil. Have regard for good*
> *things in the sight of all men. If it is possible, as*
> *much as depends on you, live peaceably with all*
> *men. Beloved, do not avenge yourselves, but*
> *rather give place to wrath; for it is written,*
> *"Vengeance is Mine, I will repay," says the Lord."*
> *(Rom. 12:17-19).*

Finally, make sure you compensate for the lack of a spouse with a healthy and supportive environment. There are other parents and friends and family members who can bring balance into your childrearing. If you are not a good disciplinarian, enlist the help of others who are. If you are not nurturing enough, learn from those who are especially good at nurturing. Children were not designed to be reared purely by the wisdom of one person, they need a healthy community to balance their growth. Please don't feel that you have to bring up your child by yourself.

CONCLUSION

So what happened to the little girl at the beginning of this chapter? As we sat down and worked through a few issues in the marriage, we discovered something very important. First, we found out that Mom favored the oldest daughter a little bit over the second one. Next, Dad favored the second daughter to make up for her being second. The rest of the dynamics are not important, since Dad and Mom committed to refocus on their marriage by making *their* relationship the priority.

These parents wisely sat down with the girls and apologized for communicating that everyone was on an equal par in the family. Dad explained that he loved Mom more than he loved the girls, but that he loved each of the girls in the same special way. Mom did the same thing, and both parents gave the girls permission to love Mom as much as Dad, and Dad as much as Mom.

Within a very short period of time, and without any further actions, the "hair pulling" of the second daughter went away and never returned. Also, just to press the point, the second daughter went up to her Dad the next day after the apology session and said, "Daddy, tell me again why you love Mommy more than you love me." She knew she was on equal par with Mom, which meant Mom and Dad's relationship was not the special one in that family.

It is a plain fact, as illustrated here; when our marriage relationship isn't the top priority, it can literally make our children pull their hair out.

8

Questions and Answers

The following is a collection of questions and answers offered in some form or another by real parents as they have worked through the principles in this book. The hope is that this section will help clarify how to apply these principles.

You told us in Chapter 1 about your son, Tripp, having a nervous habit. What happened?

I began from his birth teaching Tripp that he had the power to choose, that is, to make a decision for himself. It took root when he, as a thumb-sucker and blanket-carrier, made a decision. At about three years old, he mentioned that he wanted to get a dog. I simply told him that he could get a dog when he had quit sucking his thumb and had given up his "bahs" (his word for the cloth diapers he carried around when he sucked his thumb). The very next day, he walked up to his mother with his pile of bahs and told her that she could have them and that he had decided to quit sucking his thumb. From that day forward, he never asked for another bah, and never sucked his thumb again. He made a decision.

In the opening example, I simply reminded him of his ability to make a choice. We agreed that he could no longer scratch his ears and nose as a nervous tic. I offered him the choice of removing the habit from his life in his own way, or letting me decide on a way to remove the habit. I emphasized to him that it was his choice. He said that he would like to try it his way first, and from that day on we never saw him touch his nose or ears again. Most of us don't believe that our children have the freedom to make choices because we have grown up in such a victim mentality culture. Blame is in and responsibility is out. Common sense parents begin, as soon as possible, to help their child discover the incredible gift of his own ability to make decisions and choices.

One caution here. We don't want to completely give over all choices to our children. Rather, we can give them choices and consequences to choose between such that when a negative consequence befalls them, they can only blame themselves. I begin telling all of my children at around three years old that they can literally never get another spanking in their lives, but that it is strictly their choice. If they will do good, they will not be spanked. If they do bad, then they very well may be spanked. Please don't let your child make all the decisions in the world for his own life, especially when he is younger. If you do, your child will eat only ice cream and watch TV all day long. Instead, give him choices and consequences so that he can learn how life works and the power of self control.

Now that you mention it, what about spanking?

Spanking is a very delicate subject because it has grown so "out of vogue" in our culture. As I was writing this, I listened to "experts" sing the dangers of spanking. They say, for example, that it creates aggressiveness in children and teaches them to solve conflicts by hitting. Moreover, they suggest that it creates very unhappy and maladjusted children. This kind of reasoning is largely pseudo-intellectual theorizing, not good scientific research. I publicly challenge any legitimate researcher to interview my children and find out about their "adjustment" relative to the fact that we have employed spanking as one of our parenting tools.

Danger does exist with spanking, because it can be abused. The saying, "When the only tool you have is a hammer, you tend to treat every problem as a nail," illustrates how the abuse of spanking occurs. I will be the first to admit that many parents who use spanking use it far too often. Moreover, when spanking is not seen as a procedure to follow, but rather serves as striking out in anger, then it is not in any way a common sense tool. Our experience in our family has been that by the time the children turn four or five, we might spank them as seldom as once every other month. Once the purpose of spanking takes root in the heart of a child, actual spankings become less and less necessary.

Why do we spank? Well, the first reason is simply that the Bible teaches the appropriateness of spanking:

> "*Foolishness is bound up in the heart of a child;
> but the rod of correction will drive it far from
> him*" (Prov. 22:15), or
> "*Do not withhold correction from a child, for if
> you beat him with a rod, he will not die*"
> (Prov. 23:13).

A further study of the Scriptures would also indicate that the "back" of a child is the midway point, meaning the bottom or fanny. The rear end physiologically has been perfectly designed by God to receive spankings without damaging the body. In no sense should anyone ever hit a child in any other place than the rear end. Moreover, a paddle or flexible piece of plastic (e.g. a spatula) is better to use for one simple reason. You can hurt your hand!

The second reason that spanking has value is that it brings in a consequence immediately to young children (toddlers and older) when natural consequences cannot occur rapidly enough for learning. In other words, when your older child leaves his bike in the driveway, it is easy enough to put the bike up for a day, which in turn connects the consequence to the action. Stubbornly refusing to put toys in a box really has no consequence that a small child can connect to the event. When, however after a warning, the child's refusal brings on a spanking, then that child can learn that his disobedience is not encouraged.

The procedure that Joanna and I have used for spanking is as follows. When one of our children has clearly not obeyed an instruction that he is capable of following, then we take the child directly to a room alone so that no other children are witnesses to the event. Next, especially with younger children, we pull down the pants and rap the bottom from one to five times, depending on the severity of the offense. While the child cries, we hold him without overly comforting him. Gently, we tell the child that "that's enough crying," and follow it with this question. "Why did you get a spanking?" At first, they are not very good at articulating the answer, so we will help them, but after a while they begin to learn to identify what they did wrong. The reason we ask this question after spanking them is that it is too tempting for a child to engage you in discussion and debate to get out of a spanking. After clarifying with the child the reason for the spanking, we then pray, especially seeking to lay the issue to rest that we might go on with our day. After praying with the child, we say to him, "I love you." Usually, the child affirms his love for us too. Only once when I asked Tripp if he loved me did he respond with "No." I simply gave him the answer my friend Lee Thompson gave his son. "Well, I'm really sorry you don't love me. I guess we'll just sit here until you love me again." Shortly, Tripp smiled and said, "I love you again, Daddy." Then off he went to play.

Spanking, using this procedure, makes it a full process to bring a clear consequence to your child for failing to obey. With consistency, this becomes a part of his understanding and respect for you as a parent.

There are two basic dangers with this approach. First, you must work to never spank your child while angry. Have the child sit in his room alone until you have calmed down, but please don't get caught up in a rage while disciplining. Spanking works best when it is a very "matter of fact" consequence for failing to obey. The second problem occurs with parents who are not interacting enough with their children. If your child is not getting enough attention from you and the "I love you" part of spanking procedure is too comforting, then children will sometimes endure the pain of a spanking for the pleasure of the comfort. Comfort, in this process, should also be largely matter of fact and not overdone.

Finally, it is conceivable to raise your children without spanking. Using spanking, however, in the way we've described, is profoundly wise and effective in helping your child change in the early years. If the way you are spanking your child is not working, then quit, as I have sometimes advised parents. If you have not tried this described procedure, just watch what happens when you do. Bear in mind, a true spanking is not a magic swat from you, but the complete submission of the child to the process. It is not a true spanking if your child is running away while you try to spank.

Now, one last piece of advice. I believe it is unwise to spank children after they turn twelve. If spanking has not served its purpose by then, then it will have little effect as they begin to grow toward adulthood. In fact, the testosterone in your male child will begin to interpret spankings as a challenge, not as discipline. Please just work at getting more creative after the twelfth birthday.

It seems that we are so close to the situation that we can't really objectively see what the problem is and in what ways we are encouraging our child's actions? What do you do when you are stuck and can't figure out how you are encouraging the bad behavior?

The experience of being "stuck" is part of your learning process as a parent. If you are stuck, keep looking. It may take a day or two or a week, but if you will continue to believe that there are actions in the family that are encouraging the bad behavior, then you will find them. If you ask the right questions, your brain will find answers. In large measure, what is required here is discipline on your part to endure in the process of gaining wisdom and objectivity. You have this capacity, but it may be very much out of shape and dormant inside of you. Give it a chance. If you solve your own problem within your family rather than going to an expert or anyone else outside of your family, you will be changed forever as a parent. I suspect parents applying common sense principles often make the most simple and fatal mistake of all: they quit too soon. If you really get desperate and feel that you have given yourself enough time, then look for an older parent who has made it work in his own family. Invite this person or the couple to brainstorm with you about your situation and the Four Magic Questions that you are apply-ing to it. Frankly, my experience has been that most of the time when parents feel "stuck," they have not yet sat down and worked through the Four Magic Questions.

What about temper tantrums and whining, and other such actions?

It may seem unbelievable, and perhaps my fifth child will prove to be the exception, but we have never seen a real tem-per tantrum in our family. I personally don't believe that there is a temper tantrum gene that we missed out on by a stroke of fate. Rather, I believe that temper tantrums are the most graphic illustration of the principle "if you see it, it's encouraged." Temper tantrums occur because of the way parents react to the first small tantrum. If your child throws a fit in a grocery store and you hush him by giving him a piece of candy, isn't it clear that you are teaching him to have tantrums? Of course, it may not be candy. It may be speak-ing softly to him and taking him out of the room. If the child wanted to leave the room, then the tantrum has been rewarded. Ignoring a tantrum, walking away from a tantrum, and interrupting the tantrum with a swat on the rear are all ways not to reward a fit. I believe the reason we have never seen tantrums is that when our babies (toddler and earlier) began to have anything close to a fit or crying spell, we sim-ply placed them in their crib with the instructions that "if you're going to cry, it's okay, but you need to do it here in your bed and not disrupt the whole family with it." We also always made a point of letting them cry it out, and as soon as they stopped and were calm, we brought them back out with the family to play. Sometimes we repeated this process a number of times before it took hold. Our goal was to teach the child that his fits will not be rewarded, however, we in no way wanted to communicate that it is illegal to "cry" in our family.

Whining is another issue, however, for the Lybrands. Tripp, our first child, developed a serious problem with whining. After becoming frustrated enough with the sound "eh-eh-eh" in a very high pitched nasal tone, I stayed home one day just to watch how this whining was being encouraged. As you might guess Joanna, as a busy young mother, was not listening to Tripp's first request for necessities such as a drink of water. Every time he reached the whining stage, she turned and attended to his need, but never reprimanded his whining. In effect, he had simply been taught to whine, because whining communicated. Whenever you see a whining child, you know that the child has been taught to whine and can as easily be taught not to whine. Recently, we were waiting at the airport for Joanna to get home from a trip. We had a little time to enjoy all of the other children waiting for parents to arrive. At one point, a little boy lay down on the floor and began crying and pounding his fist on the carpet. I pulled my children together and pointed at this little boy and said, "Now, watch. A parent is going to come and pick up this child and kiss him and carry him back to a chair." I did not know who this child belonged to, but as predicted, out of nowhere came Mom, who picked up this crying child and further reinforced his behavior.

All of this sounds a lot like manipulation, or bribing. What is the difference?

I see a big difference between manipulating and bribing, and influencing and teaching. There is no doubt that we are bringing to bear our influence on our children to encourage them to develop habits, behaviors, and ways of thinking that will serve them well throughout their lives. Manipulation and bribery largely have to do with the motives, as well as the methods behind the actions. Manipulation carries with it the idea of shrewd and devious influence, centering a focus on personal gain. Bribery also has to do with gaining influence for corrupt and self-serving purposes. When we as parents are training our children, we are using common sense methods to influence their growth and development. We, as parents, have the best shot at proper motives for our children. The fact is that your child will be "manipulated" by something. It may be the television or corrupt friends, but he will be influenced. Do you believe that the motives and goals of friends and society are so selfless and morally pure that their influence should surpass your own? We are attempting to bring our influence to bear on certain behaviors and ideas for the purpose of helping the child own or internalize the behavior for himself when we put up stickers and give a jelly bean during potty training. Our goal is not to get him to eat his jelly bean every time he uses the restroom, nor are we trying to get him to "go potty" so that we can brag to our friends. Rather, we are seeking to help him develop independence so that he can learn within himself to care for himself. The same holds for the teen who gets to use the car after the yard is mowed or the room is clean. I believe many of us as parents do manipulate and bribe our children, because we are seeking to get them to "leave us alone," and therefore our motives are selfish. When we can apply sound principles to help our child change in order to develop him into a sound citizen and meaningful contributor to the world, then it is not manipulation, it is training.

I have a problem with being consistent, and sometimes it's just because I am too tired. How can I overcome this problem?

Inconsistency and tiredness are usually a sign that your child or children are somewhat "out of control." I don't mean that we as parents don't get tired, but if the state is constant exhaustion, then something surely is wrong. Consistency usually comes when both parents participate in the child training process. With both parents, you are able to keep one another encouraged and accountable. Usually, the problem of staying consistent comes from a parent who is too consumed with meeting the child's needs and making sure the child "likes" him or her. One of my professors at Dallas Theological Seminary, Dr. Howard Hendricks, has often said, "When you do something for someone that he can do for himself, then you make an emotional cripple of him." Chances are, unfortunately, that if you are inconsistent, you are somehow being encouraged to be inconsistent. Remember, if you see it, it is encouraged. The best idea I have for consistency is for you to take the Four Magic Questions and apply them to your inconsistency. You may find a very simple solution such as telling your children that every time they get you to do something for them that they can do themselves, you will give them a dollar bill. I suspect, unless you think so little of money, that you will change your consistency problem rapidly.

What about children with attention deficit disorder (ADD)?

I can't enter into such a complicated debate in a question and answer session, but I will observe that ADD is a very unclear diagnosis. There is no real test that we can administer to know whether a child has ADD. It usually requires an "expert" who can spend enough time with the child and in the family to gain a history to determine the validity of the problem.

What does seem to be consistent concerning ADD is that the environment in which the child grows is a crucial ingredient. Children are resilient and adaptable, including children with ADD. Sadly, because of the lost art of common sense parenting, many of the children in our society are simply active and undisciplined. I believe the principles that we have shared in this book apply as readily to ADD children as they do to any others. The standards, however, may need to be a little different. Realistic behaviors and expectations for your child are crucial. Creating an environment and reward structure that encourages your child to behave within appropriate boundaries should be your goal. The key distinction with ADD children is that they are often slower at internalizing a consistent habit or behavior. Like all children, an ADD child has a struggle largely around the issue of motivation. An ADD child who is truly motivated to do something will get it done. Setting up an environment through the four questions will aid you greatly in bringing about the behaviors you want in your child. The greatest danger I see with parents who have accepted the ADD label is that they sometimes believe they are victims and can do nothing to influence and develop their child. This is simply not true. The one thing you might want to keep in mind is that your child may require more immediate (not long term) rewards or consequences for his or her behavior than you are used to giving. Additionally, you will probably find that removing something your child already has (a Nintendo, part of his allowance, etc.) for failing to obey will be more effective than trying to find a reward that he can earn.

My personal conviction is that if parents who have accepted the ADD label would see the situation as an issue of their child's unique personality instead of simply a problem, then the way in which the child can be approached is much more effective. It is prudent to learn to "treat each child the same by treating each one differently." That is, each of your children is unique. Good parenting involves helping your child learn to make use of his strengths and buttress his weaknesses. We all have both, but we make our best contributions through the things at which we excel. Strengths are found in what your child has a "knack" for, that is, it comes easy to him. Also, a true talent is used for the benefit of others. Please build on those good things in your child.

When is it too late to help my child change?

It is always too late when you have given up. It is also too late when your child has left home and refuses to look to you for advice. The real question has to do with our changing roles as parents. When your child begins to hit his later teenage years (about sixteen and up), he will be trying to answer and settle upon his identity or "who he is." This stage is really the last shot parents have to overcome any of the mistakes made earlier. The best advice I have for dealing with a child at this late stage is to learn to view him as a pre-adult. You can still apply the Four Magic Questions, but apply them as to a person who is moving toward adulthood, not as a person who has just left childhood. Your oppressive mothering and fathering at this stage will only incite your child. I'm not saying that you shouldn't establish consequences for behaviors, but work more diligently at making sure the consequences are known up front and are understood as fair and appropriate by your child before he ever violates the rule and receives the consequence. It is more crucial at this stage, perhaps than at any other, for that young man or young woman who is still under your care and protection to see the choices he or she is making and the results that occur as intimately connected.

My spouse and I don't agree about what standards we should have for the children, or how we should approach child rearing. What do we do?

My first recommendation is to re-read Chapter 7 because the problem is obviously a relationship issue. The second recommendation is for you to apply the Four Magic

Questions to your lack of agreement. Somehow, in your system, not agreeing about the children is being encouraged. It may be a more basic issue of communication rather than agreement, meaning that the two of you may not have any idea of what each other's standards are. If you apply the Four Magic Questions, you will diagnose what's wrong and begin to find ways to encourage like-mindedness concerning your children.

How long does it take for a behavior to change?

Behaviors can change instantly, contrary to popular opinion. Whenever someone develops a phobia to a bridge, an elevator, or a dog, it occurs instantly because of that one experience. Generally, however, it usually takes from three to five days of a consistent behavior for it to begin to be internalized by most younger children. The real answer is that it will take just as long as it takes for the child to realize that his good behavior will consistently be encouraged, and his bad behavior will consistently be discouraged. Inconsistency is usually what extends the learning process. As soon as your child is convinced that things have changed and will be consistent, most likely your child will change.

We've noticed that after vacation or a visit with the grandparents, our child's behavior is much worse after he gets back home. What do we do?

The best thing to do is to accept that this is a fact of life. Vacations are almost, by definition, a disruption of the routine. Therefore, vacation encourages different behaviors from your children. In addition to vacation, grandparents have, it seems, a constitutional right to spoil children. I'm not sure I want to seek a constitutional amendment, since I hope to indulge in this as a grandparent myself someday. The key is simply to get back to the routine. Usually, this child is simply asking if the rules are still the same as when he left. He may be trying to get you to adopt the rules that the grandparents use, or that a vacation follows. It's strictly an issue of who will run the home. We have found that our children, even though they love vacation, actually look forward to getting back to the routine and safety that comes with knowing how home operates. Vacation and grandparents simply prove the principles in this book. Rest assured, nothing is permanently wrong, it just takes a little time to get back to "normal."

Will there ever be a day when we can relax and lighten up as parents?

A common response to applying these principles is that it allows you to begin to enjoy parenting. Relaxing and lightening up comes as your children develop and you begin to have confidence in your ability to parent. If you are fearful, it is difficult to relax. If you will begin to apply these principles and take note of the changes in your child, you will begin to realize that you have been well equipped as a parent. As you further develop these skills, you will be able to relax all the more. The one exception will then be your temptation to point out to other parents the mistakes they are making. Please don't run up to another parent and say, "If you see it, it's encouraged!" Wait until they ask. You will be surprised, they will ask someday.

I have a strong-willed child. Are there any special rules for him?

My personal conviction is that all children are strong-willed. Some just happen to be more "head on" in their efforts to get their own way. When your sweet, soft-spoken child wants something, and you immediately give it to her, then you are rewarding her sweetness and not finding out if she is strong-willed. It is the "no" that brings out their strong will. I'm not saying that some children are not more intense than others, but they are all self-willed and interested in getting their own way. It is that very fact that underscores the principles in this book. We are, in a sense, using their "strong will" against (for) them. By learning to encourage their behavior, we are tapping into their need to do the thing that benefits them the most. These principles apply to all children. It is, however, your unique and wise application that will make the difference.

We have a problem transferring authority to other adults and baby-sitters. What should we do?

Generally speaking, children that do not respect other adults think of themselves as adults. Use the Four Magic Questions to look at how the child has been encouraged not to respect authority, or to think of himself as an equal with adults. You might also want to look at the authorities in your own lives, such as your boss, relationship between husband and wife, or respect for leaders within your church. If you, as a parent, are contemptuous towards authorities in your life, what does that encourage in your child? Applying the Magic Questions to obeying a baby-sitter should rapidly give you a solution to apply in your own situation. Somehow, the child has been encouraged to rebel against adults and authority. When you adjust the environment to encourage their respect for authority, your child will probably change quickly.

Our children are constantly at each other's throats, and I feel like I am always having to play the role of judge between their disputes. What should I do?

One common sense theory of sibling rivalry is that it is simply a part of how we learn to communicate and cooperate as human beings. In other words, childhood is training and a certain amount of sibling rivalry should be expected.

Beyond a tolerable range, however, most sibling rivalry is, as you might expect, encouraged inside the family system. When a parent gets into the role of being a "judge," then it is guaranteed that the rivalry is being encouraged. If, for example, you often hear the phrase "Mom, brother won't let me play with the (blank)" then very likely you have consistently rewarded this behavior by going to brother and making him share. If you could, instead, begin to think about how to encourage the children to solve their own problems, you would see something entirely different happen. Joanna first showed me this when youngsters came over to play and they would begin to fight over a toy. Joanna would simply pick up the toy and say, "Well, obviously you two can't play with this," and she would put it up on a very high shelf. After a few times, the children learned to sort out how to share because the toy would go away if they fought. Naturally, a mild risk is run here in that one child could start a fight in order to get the other child not to play with it. Discernment and wisdom is in constant demand on our part as parents. I personally have found it very effective to warn the children of their need to solve the issue among themselves and to tell them the consequence if they do not. With very few exceptions, the children, once they understand this system, begin to resolve things between themselves. The key is to focus on punishing or disciplining both for a conflict, though it may seem one-sided. We don't need to assume that just because one is the noisiest that the other child did not play a role in the conflict. In essence, this follows very much the same pattern we have seen throughout the book. Their rivalry is being encouraged, and oftentimes because Mom or Dad is playing the role of arbitrator. Give the problem back to the children and give them the gift of learning to resolve problems between themselves.

Sometimes my child has a violent outlash of anger toward me. What is going on, and what should I do?

Usually, violent outlashes of anger have been slowly taught over time such that what began as a small outburst was somehow encouraged in the child to become a greater one. Normally, it is a parent's reaction to the anger that is the key. If you will objectively look at your reaction when the child is angry, try to interpret it as a reward or a way in which you are accidentally encouraging your child to use anger as a tool to get you to do what he wants. In general, the answer to the earlier question concerning tantrums should be considered since tantrums are a form of angry outbursts.

What about the problem of repeated "minor" acts of disobedience?

Minor acts of disobedience are simply a matter of where a parent will draw the line or establish a standard. An obvious example is when we begin to "count" for our children to obey us. We teach the child that the number three or the number five is when we "really mean business." Choosing the number three or the number five or the number ten is arbitrary. You could just as easily develop a standard that we have implemented in our home of first time obedience. In other words, we have focused on getting the children to obey us the first time we ask them to do something. This may sound rigid, and you will have to establish your own standards for your family. I believe, however, there have been many children saved from death, because when in a dangerous situation they obeyed instantly. They were told to sit down and stay, or come back to mother, or get out of the street, and since they immediately obeyed, they avoided the oncoming harm. Minor acts of disobedience simply indicate that the system encourages or tolerates the minor acts of disobedience, while not tolerating and not encouraging major acts of disobedience. In large measure, it is simply an issue of what your personal standards will be, and how well you work at seeing the appropriate behaviors encouraged. In applying the Four Magic Questions, I suggest you focus especially on Question 2, "What do I want to see?" Do you want to see your child disobeying minor things, or do you want to see your child obeying when you give him directions?

What about when my child's behavior is good, but his attitude is ugly?

Very much like the previous question, the issue concerns your own standards in your family. We have sought not to encourage bad attitudes, but good ones from which flow good actions. Since the children were little, we have had a policy that if your attitude is really bad, or you are very, very unhappy, you may go into your room and stay there until you decide to have a good attitude and to carry happiness with you. On some occasions, before we have gone on an outing as a family, one of the children has had a "bad attitude." I communicated to him in plenty of time that he will not go on the trip until his attitude is straightened up; and that he had best begin to work on it now because we are leaving in thirty minutes. I certainly believe you should seek to encourage both good behavior and good attitudes. P.S. You better realize that you must fulfill the consequence you promise. Our children know I would gladly sacrifice their trip one time to have joy from then on!

My child often makes me repeat my questions and answers, almost to the point of nagging. It's like he won't take "No" for an answer. What do I do?

Whenever children ask us to continually repeat questions and refuse to take "no" for an answer, it is much the same as debating and arguing with us. The only way a child continually argues with a parent is if the parent will engage in argument. In other words, continuing to debate with your child encourages the child to debate with you because there might be a chance that you will give in. Most probably you have given in, and therefore have encouraged the child to debate. Not to be redundant, but applying the Magic Questions to this issue will give you both insight as to how it has been caused, and a plan for how to cure it.

What do we do about our child getting a "Yes" from Dad, but then separately getting a "No" from Mom?

This question probably originated with Cain and Abel, and is often a simple strategy on the child's part to "divide and conquer." Usually, this occurs because it has worked in the past for the child. If you and your spouse will figure a way for this not to work, then it should go away. For example, you might simply have a rule concerning the kinds of requests that require both Mom and Dad's approval. Once this is understood, then you and your spouse will necessarily have to talk for the decision to be made. Other decisions are best left to one or the other parent as he or she is available. Usually, this particular problem gets caught consistently, except when the child engages in lying by, for example, saying, "Well, Dad said I could (when he didn't) if you said it's OK." Lying consistently definitely occurs when it is encouraged by succeeding. I strongly encourage you to make it a standard that no lying be tolerated in your home.

Sometimes my child is "selectively deaf," that is, he won't listen to my instructions. What do I do?

First of all, sometimes our children become self-protective and don't listen because we tend to give them long and involved lectures. These lectures truly do fall on deaf ears. Also, not listening can be encouraged by re-explaining instructions until your child obeys. I personally have not experienced a deafness problem with my children, however, I have noticed on occasion that Joanna does experience this problem. I have also watched her wisely notice that vision and hearing are connected. In other words, she first makes sure the child looks at her directly, and then she communicates. It is usually the case that selective deafness is accompanied by the child looking somewhere else. In addition to this, you may want to think through how you could encourage active listening by understanding and applying the principles we have discussed, especially with the use of the Four Magic Questions.

Sometimes my child uses rebellious or attention-getting behavior, such as not showing respect to others, not showing good manners, or talking too loudly to distract others. How can I get these to go away?

In large measure, these kinds of behaviors are best treated by the principles in this book. As you understand the principles and apply the Magic Questions to each of these behaviors, you will very likely see them go away in a short period of time. I especially need to emphasize that it is crucial to find a replacement behavior. In other words, the issue is not to move from "talking loudly" to "not talking at all." Instead, you want to teach your child to talk softly or properly in a certain context. The goal is not to have no manners, but to have good manners. Manners, in particular, require practice. Having a child go out of the room and come back into the room to properly and politely interrupt a conversation between adults is the best way he is going to learn it. As they say in football, "run that play until you get it right."

How are these principles different from what has been traditionally called behavior modification?

In a way, there is no difference. One of the common recommendations for newlyweds is to first have a dog before having children. The idea is that as you learn about care and training, it will prepare you for having children. Children, however, because they are human beings, do not respond perfectly to Pavlovian conditioning. They are, however, greatly influenced by rewards and punishment for behaviors. In general, the younger a child is the more readily behavior modification can be directly applied. As a child grows, however, it is less effective. The reason for this is simple. Children, as human beings, have a will. Your child, despite everything you offer to encourage a certain behavior, can still choose against you. The ability to choose is one of the most treasured and hated aspects of our humanity. Treasured because it separates us from animals. Hated because people often do not choose to do what we want them to. Your focus as a parent is to create an environment that encourages the development of good behavior and good values. The traditional sense of behavior modification is only a small part of what explains human behavior. Furthermore, a purist in the use of behavior modification really has no way to understand the dignity of our humanity in having been given a will, the ability to choose, by God.

One final addition to this answer is found in the importance of understanding the family as a system. The principles in this book have been designed to allow you to work on changes within the family system without understanding all the dynamics involved. I have truly tried to take a common sense approach. Family systems center around the idea that all of us in a family "fit" together in certain important ways. Affecting one person in the family affects everyone. Much like a child's mobile over his crib, pulling down on one side raises the other. Normally, when you find a "demon" in a family, you find an "angel," as well. There is a kind of balancing act that is working in the system, and healthier families develop a healthier balance. Behavior modification focuses on a narrow part of how people develop and learn, whereas thinking in terms of family systems embraces the larger context concerning growth and change. I have attempted to offer a more common sense approach, which considers these issues and much more in seeking to help your child change without your child's help.

If we apply the principles in this book perfectly, does it guarantee that our children will turn out well?

The hardest thing for us to admit as parents is that no matter how well we do, our children can turn out "bad." It is important to appreciate this fact, because it is the only way that children who grow up in "bad" homes could ever turn out "good." I emphasized in the last question the importance of the dignity involved in having a will, or the ability to choose as a human being. The fact is that good homes do sometimes produce bad children, and bad homes do sometimes produce good children. We are concerned here with principles. Principles are normally true, but can have exceptions or be overridden by a higher principle. The best chance of your children turning out well is if you have a healthy marriage and provide common sense principles to developing your child toward adulthood. There is no guarantee, because your child can choose to reject all of his "training." If you ignore common sense and provide an environment that leaves the child to train himself, then you greatly increase the likelihood that he will turn out poorly. Plato stated it for nations when he observed, "**What's honored in a country is cultivated there.**" Proverbs 29:15 states it for the family. "*The rod and rebuke give wisdom, but a child left to himself brings shame to his mother.*"

Don't, however, underestimate your influence and responsibility. If you can't be blamed if your child turns out bad, then you can't take credit if he turns out good. The fact is, common sense tells us that your child deserves credit as well, for making his own choices. The role of a common sense parent, to your credit, is to give your child the best shot at making good choices. "If you encourage it, you will see it!"

CONCLUSION

"Every great example takes hold of us with the authority of a miracle, and says to us, 'If ye had but faith, ye could do the same things.'"

— Jacobi

If the Parenting Revolution ever takes root and helps create the changes we so desperately need in these times, it will largely be because of the power of example. If you have the courage to pursue wisdom and become an example of common sense for others, there is no predicting how powerful and strategic the sequence of influence through you will be.

It all begins at home. God's blessings in the spirit of James 4:8.

Epilogue

SOMETIMES COMMON SENSE NEEDS HELP

In the effort to return the skills and permission to parent to mothers and fathers throughout this nation, I in no way mean to suggest that parents never need help. Some parents can become clearly unfit to parent. Others can become entangled in such a fishnet of problems that there is no way out without help.

If you are overwhelmed and still have no idea where to start, or your problems are so great as to be beyond you, then please seek help.

I'm not suggesting that you simply defer to an expert, but find a person or persons who can help you discern and apply solutions for the problems you face. Should it be a psychologist? A social worker? Another parent? A pastor? I can't answer that question for you. Any of these individuals could be of help provided they can answer "yes" to one simple question: Has their approach to parenting resulted in basically healthy and productive children?

There are no guarantees in this world, but there is a better chance that you can receive some helpful common sense from someone who has made it work. If your "counselor" is unwilling to answer this question, then find another one. No one worth his salt will be insulted. No matter the knowledge the person possesses, if he hasn't made it work, it is likely that he doesn't understand how to parent. There may be exceptions, but they are not worth the gamble.

Ideally, I recommend you find a church committed to helping the family. This strategy will provide the right environment to apply sound advice. Finally, the best way to find a counselor is to look for healthy and productive children. If you find them, just follow them home to their parents. I predict you'll find a person with insight for your situation that will never be captured in a book or a seminar. You'll find the true expert: A Wise and Revolutionary Parent, the essence of Common Sense.

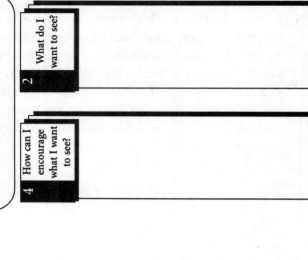

The 4 Magic Questions WORKSHEET

1. What do I see?
2. What do I want to see?
3. How am I encouraging what I see?
4. How can I encourage what I want to see and discourage all else?

1 What do I see?

3 How am I encouraging what I see?

5 How can I discourage what I see?

INSTRUCTIONS:
1. Choose one behavioral problem
2. Start with STEP #1 and continue *in order by STEPS* (#1, #2, #3, etc.)
3. If you aren't satisfied with your answers, try again after 1-2 days of reflection
4. Go to page 2

2 What do I want to see?

4 How can I encourage what I want to see?

Worksheet (p.2)

Try limiting A and B below to only one or two items

What do I want to see? (STEP #2)

_____
_____
_____
_____

A) How will I discourage what I don't want to see (STEP # 5)

_____
_____
_____
_____

B) How will I encourage what I want to see? (STEP # 4)

_____
_____
_____
_____

C) In one week on _____, I will evaluate how much progress has been made, and re-think my plan if necessary.

Notes

1. This definition of wisdom is modified from in-class discussions with my friend and mentor, Dr. Elliot Johnson, professor of Bible Exposition at Dallas Theological Seminary.

2. Charles "Chic" Thompson, *What a Great Idea! The Key Steps Creative People Take*, (New York: Harper Perennial, 1992) pp. 66-69.

3. Michael LeBoeuf, *How to Win Customers and Keep Them for Life*, (New York: The Putnam Publishing Group).

4. Ibid.

5. George Bernard Shaw, Pygmalion: A Romance in Five Acts (New York: Penguin, 1993).

6. Barbara Dafoe Whitehead, "Divorce and Kids: The Evidence Is In." *Reader's Digest*, 143, no. 855 (July 1993): p.118-123.

For Further Study

Since I have intentionally avoided trying to tell you what your standards for your children should be, you may truly want some help finding out what good standards are for your children. In this kind of an instance, experts can serve a purpose, as long as you don't simply defer to their ideas. The following four resources have been extremely helpful in my own life, in our local church, or in the lives of people I deeply respect. I highly recommend these resources if you are interested in further study.

Ezzo, Gary & Marie
  Growing Families International
  9259 Eton Avenue
  Chatsworth, CA 91311
  1-818-772-6264

Fugate, J. Richard, *What the Bible Says About...Child Training*. Tempe, Arizona: Aletheia
  Division of Alpha Omega Publications. 1980.

Howe, Dr. Marlin
  Hope For The Family
  3405 Pine Valley Drive
  North Little Rock, AK 72120-1771
  1-800-999-4673

Moore, Raymond and Dorothy. *Home Built Discipline*.
  Nashville, Tennessee: Thomas Nelson, Inc. 1987.

About the Author

Hometown: Anniston, Alabama

Education: University of Alabama, B.A. English Literature
Dallas Theological Seminary, Masters Biblical
Studies, with Honor

Current Position: Pastor, Midland Bible Church,
Midland, Texas

Previous Works: *Heavenly Citizenship*, Treasure House

Your Comments and Success Stories are Welcome

Please feel free to write with your comments or successes implementing the principles in this book. Your stories may be shared with others for their encouragement and to help advance the Parenting Revolution!

Also, Fred Lybrand is available for a limited number of speaking engagements and seminars upon request and availability. You may contact him through

The B & B
MEDIA
Group

1200 Lexington Square
Corsicana, TX   75110

1-800-927-0517 ext. 13

Additional Resources

- **4 Magic Questions WORKSHEET** - A laminated, color, & re-usable fullsized worksheet to help your child change by targeting key behaviors. Great for the refrigerator as a clear and constant reminder! **$ 4.00**

- **Heavenly Citizenship:** *The Spiritual Alternative to Power Politics,* Fred R. Lybrand Jr., Treasure House **$ 7.95**

  This is a book that ought to be read by Christians who want to live in a distinctive fashion in today's world.

  Elliot E. Johnson, Professor of Bible Exposition
  Dallas Theological Seminary

  This is foundational material to spiritual growth and to keeping a clear focus on God's program for His people...a warning to all Christians about their spiritual priorities.

  Alexander Strauch, Author, Biblical Eldership

- **Communication:** *A Biblical View* **$ 20.00**

  This 7 Part Audio Cassette Series is designed to offer a **NEW** way to understand and think about communication and productivity... whether at work, home, church, or in day-to-day relationships. Learn what's wrong with communication from God's view and how to fix it His way.

To Order:
Call 1-800-927-0517 ext. 13
or write
P.O. Box 51553
Midland, TX   79710-1553